DAILY QUOTES
WITH QUERIES FOR REFLECTION

EDITED BY ROSALIE V. GRAFE

Quaker Abbey Press, LLC

Daily Quotes with Queries for Reflection
Edited by Rosalie V. Grafe

Copyright 2011, Rosalie V. Grafe
Available online at quakerabbeypress.com

ISBN 978-0-9820035-5-8   0-9820035-5-2

For CIP, contact Library of Congress

Cover design by the Editor based on *Très Riches Heures du Duc de Berry*

Photo of Carl Enoch William Leonard Dahlstrom, Ph.D. (CEWLD), Portland State *Viking*, 1955, used by permission.

Dedicated by the Editor to her friends at the Northumbria Community. Find them online at: northumbriacommunity.org.

Rosalie V. Grafe

THE QUOTES

E xcept as noted, the literary quotes are selected by subject from 9,000 entries in a boxed collection—copied by hand onto 4x7 index cards during his 50 years of teaching Humanities—by Dr. Carl E. W. L. Dahlstrom (1897–1981) author of *Sent to Hell From Ann Arbor: A College Student's World War One*. The Bible verses are from *The Holy Bible: Authorized Version*, Edited by Rev. C.I. Scofield, D.D., New, Improved Edition, Oxford University Press, 1945.

TABLE OF CONTENTS

⇜JANUARY⇝

JANUARY 1

Isaiah 54:1

1 Sing, O barren, thou that didst not bear; break forth into singing, and cry aloud, thou that didst not travail with child: for more are the children of the desolate than the children of the married wife, saith the LORD.

Obituary (Epitaph)

My ship now dives the darkling deep
And rudders for the bottom's rot,
And Like all ships that sailed before,
My own will soon be quite forgot.

CEWLD

Query: Is Down ever mistaken for Up? How do we course-correct?

JANUARY 2

Psalm 25:16

16 Turn thee unto me, and have mercy upon me; for I am desolate and afflicted.

Death Complex

'…Enki-du, my brother whom I loved, the end of mortality has overtaken him. I wept for him seven days and nights till the worm fastened on him. Because of my brother I am afraid of death, because of my brother I stray through the wilderness and cannot rest.' (Gilgamesh speaking.)

N.K. Sanders
The Epic of Gilgamesh,

Baltimore, Penguin, 1973, p. 101

Query: Does our finding of Meaning matter outside the boundaries of our own skin?

JANUARY 3

Mark 4:21–23

21 And he said unto them, Is a candle brought to be put under a bushel, or under a bed? And not to be set on a candlestick?
22 For there is nothing hid, which shall not be manifested; neither was anything kept secret, but that it should come abroad.
23 If any man have ears to hear, let him hear.

Life

An invisible force compels me to walk a stretch of the road; my head bowed or held high, alone or at another's side—and we call that life. I look back, and we call that conscience. Someone smiles at me and gives me his hand, and we call that love. Someone offers me his support and complicity and we speak of friendship. I close my eyes, and that is called questioning. And then if one finds oneself a few steps ahead, a few encounters later, at the side of the road, at the entrance to night, at the edge of the precipice, one says 'That's it, it's over.' And all the wealth of this existence, all the mystery of the 'I' [*ich, Jag, ila, ego, io*] vanishes in one sweep: a man has lived.

Elie Wiesel,
The Oath (1973),
New York, Avon, 1974, pp. 78–79
[Square brackets in quote are supplied by CEWLD, Ed.]

Query: Can we love and let go…of life?

JANUARY 4

Genesis 43:14

14 …If I am bereaved of my children, I am bereaved.

Death Complex

[Gilgamesh to Urshanabi, "the ferryman of Utnapishtim"…similar to Charon, the ferryman on the Styx, the river separating the living from the dead.]

His fate lies heavy upon me. How can I be silent, how can I rest? He is dust and I too shall die and be laid in the earth forever. I am afraid of death, therefore, Urshanabi, tell me which is the road to Utnapishtim? If it is possible I will cross the waters of death; if not, I will wander still farther through the wilderness.

N.K.Sanders,
The Epic of Gilgamesh, Second Revised Edition,
Baltimore, Penguin, 1973, p. 101

Query: How can we hear the groaning at the world's heart and go on with our daily rounds? How can we not?

JANUARY 5

II Samuel 15:30

30 And David went up by the ascent of Mt. Olivet, and wept as he went up, and had his head covered, and went barefoot, and all the people that were with him covered every man his head, weeping as they went up.

Soul and Consciousness

The idea of soul or souls as functional parts of human beings has been common at least since the Egyptian concepts of the *ka* and *la*. We find so-called archaic societies with concepts of many souls for one body.

To what extent is the 'soul' concept the beginning of a new consciousness? Is, for example, the Christian concept of soul in any respect related to the consciousness that bursts upon the Near East and the Mediterranean area around the first millennium B.C.?

CEWLD

Query: Do we speak to our dead? Do they respond?

JANUARY 6

Luke 2:19

19 But Mary kept all these things and pondered them in her heart.

Soul—Reality of

The self-generating power of the soul is man's true and final secret, by virtue of which he is made in the likeness of God the creator and distinguished from all living things. These images, ideas, values and potentialities of the treasure hidden in the unconscious are brought to birth and realized by the hero in his [sic] various guises—savior and man of action, seer and sage, founder and artist, inventor and discoverer, scientist and leader.

Erich Newmann,
The Origins and History of Consciousness,
Princeton, N.J., 1971, pp. 210-211

Query: Can we remain silent until our words are "in due season"?

JANUARY 7

Psalm 15:3

3 Consider and hear me O LORD my God: lighten my eyes lest I sleep the sleep of death.

Pain

Nothing justifies the pain [one] man causes another.

Elie Wiesel,
The Oath (1973),
New York, Avon, 1974, p. 147

Query: Who can be with another, be truly "with" in devastating sorrow?

In what manner do we turn aside from their need?

JANUARY 8

Psalm 69:8

8 I am become a stranger unto my brethren, and an alien unto my mother's children.

Famine (Medieval)

Famine, particularly before the twelfth century, was frequent, and one chronicler tells us that in a very bad year human flesh was on sale in the market.

Marjorie Rowlong,
Life in Medieval Times, 1968,
New York, Capricorn, 1973, p. 46

Query: If we have faith without seeing a path back to hope in this life, how far can we continue?

JANUARY 9

Deuteronomy 8:3

3 And he humbled thee, and suffered thee to hunger, and fed thee with manna, which thou knewest not, neither did thy fathers know; that he might make thee know that man doth not live by bread only, but by every word that proceedeth out of the mouth of the LORD doth man live.

Wretchedness

From a letter of Bertrand Russell to Lowes Dickinson, July 19, 1903:

Why should you suppose I think it foolish to wish to see the people one is fond of? What else is there to make life tolerable? We stand on the shore of an ocean crying to the night and the emptiness; sometimes a voice answers out of the darkness. But it is a voice of one drowning; and in a moment the silence returns. The world seems to me quite dreadful; the unhappiness of most people is very great, and I often wonder how they all endure it. To know people well is to know their tragedy it is usually the central thing about which their lives are built. And I suppose if they did not live most of the time in the things of the moment, they would not be able to go on.

Bertrand Russell,
The Autobiography of Bertrand Russell: Early Years 1872–WWI,
New York, Bantam, 1968, p. 251

Query: How does one break the un-endingness-perception of wretchedness in the mind of one's friend? In one's own mind?

JANUARY 10

Proverbs 25:25

25 As cold waters to a thirsty soul, so is good news from a far country.

Gossip

One of the earliest forms of jet propulsion was gossip.

CEWLD

Query: News from afar, from whom do we believe it and how does it affect our lives?

JANUARY 11

Esther 8:6

6 For how shall I endure to see the evil that shall come unto my people? or how shall I endure to see the destruction of my kindred?

Archaeologist and Archaeology

The great temples of Malta lay claim to be the world's most impressive prehistoric monuments. Like the still older megalithic tombs of Atlantic Europe, they stand out as the single great achievement of the society which created them—a society without cities or written records or any attributes of a civilization other than the monuments themselves.

Colin Renfrew,
Before Civilization,
N.Y., Knopf, 1973, p. 147

Query: When we lock the door behind us for the last time, what remains behind in the empty house?

JANUARY 12

Psalm 108:12

12 Give us help from trouble: for vain is the help of man.

Good Life, The

Too often people expect the 'good life' somehow to be available like a storehouse of supplies. It should be possible thus to acquire the good life as one buys appliances, houses, foods, clothing, etc.

The good life, however, has to be made. Note, for example, that household pets attain the feline good life by being totally selfish. Men & women are animals, but they are very special animals—human. They can attain the good human life only by sharing, cooperating, understanding, loving, by being altruistic instead of selfish.

CEWLD

Query: What do we "get" from "giving"?

JANUARY 13

Judges 5:6–7

6 In the days of Shamgar, the son of Anath, in the days of Jael, the highways were unoccupied, and the travelers walked through byways.
7 The inhabitants of villages ceased, they ceased in Israel, until that I Deborah arose, that I arose a mother in Israel.

[Note: Date given for Judges, 1296 BCE and for Ruth, 1322 BCE, Ed.]

Goodness

The one activity taught by Jesus in word and deed is the activity of goodness and goodness obviously, harbors a tendency to hide from being seen or heard. Christian [attitudes] toward the public realm, the tendency at least of early Christians to lead a life as far removed from the public realm as possible, can also be understood as self-evident consequence of devotion to good works, independent of all beliefs and expectations. For it is manifest that the moment that a good work becomes known and public, it loses its specific character of goodness, of being done for nothing but goodness' sake. When goodness appears openly, it is no longer goodness, though it may still be useful as organized charity or an act of solidarity. Therefore: 'Take heed that ye do not your alms before men, to be seen of them.' Goodness can exist only when it is not perceived, not even by its author; whoever sees himself performing a good work is no longer good, but at best a useful member of society or a dutiful member of a church. Therefore: 'Let not thy left hand know what thy right hand doeth.' It may be this curious negative quality of goodness, the lack of outward phenomenal manifestation, that makes Jesus of Nazareth's appearance in history such a profoundly paradoxical event; it certainly seems to be the reason why he thought and taught that no man can be good: 'Why callest thou me good? None is good, save one, that is, God.'

Hannah Arendt,
The Human Condition (1958),
Univ. of Chicago, 1974, pp. 73–75

Query: Why do we still mourn the lack of a thank you for a benefit given with no expectation of return?

JANUARY 14

Judges 18:10

10 When ye go, ye shall come unto a people secure, and to a large land: for God hath given it unto your hand a place where there is no want of anything that is in the earth.

Goodness and Solitude

Good works, because they must be forgotten instantly, can never become part of the world; they come and go, leaving no trace. They truly are not of this world.

It is this worldlessness inherent in good works that makes the lover of goodness an essentially religious figure and that makes goodness, like wisdom in antiquity, an essentially non-human, superhuman quality and yet love of goodness, unlike love of wisdom, is not restricted to the experiences of the few, just as loneliness, unlike solitude, is within the range of every man's experience. In a sense, therefore, goodness and loneliness are of much greater relevance to politics than wisdom and solitude; yet only solitude can become an authentic way of life in the figure of the philosopher, whereas the much more general experience of loneliness is so contradictory to the human condition of plurality that it is simply unbearable for any length of time and needs the company of God, the only imaginable witness of good works, if it is not to annihilate human existence altogether. The otherworldliness of religious experience in so far as it is truly the experience of love in the sense of an activity and not the more frequent one of beholding passively a revealed truth, manifests itself within the world itself; this, like all other activities, does not leave the world, but must be performed within it. But this manifestation, though it appears in the space where other activities are performed and depends upon it, is of an actively negative nature; fleeing the world and hiding from its inhabitants, it negates the space the world offers to men, and most of all that public part of it where everything and everybody are seen and heard by others.

Goodness, therefore, as a consistent way of life, is not only impossible within the confines of the public realm, it is even destructive of it.

Hannah Arendt,
The Human Condition, (1958),
University of Chicago, 1974, pp. 73–75, pp. 76–77

Query: Must our good works be known abroad so that God may be glorified thereby?

JANUARY 15

Hebrews 11:1

1 Now faith is the substance of things hoped for, the evidence of things not seen.

Faith

[In memory of Jocelyn Rose Latka, March 24, 1987–January 5, 2006]

Dear Rosalie,

...A repeat, that you are quite right to make your own decisions in these matters. If you have faith, it is your own—you are not likely to acquire it through any process of social osmosis, suggestion or authoritarian command.

As for myself, I can say that my wife and I ceased defining ourselves politically, religiously, aesthetically, philosophically, or any other way. We came to the conclusion that our task in this world was to learn what it meant to be decent human beings, to act on this knowledge, and to subject ourselves to correction as needed. We could not believe in an angry, vengeful God who terrorized his own creation, nor could we believe that God wished constantly to be praised like an egotistic human being. Rituals and ceremony might be aesthetically pleasing and emotionally satisfying without necessarily having anything to live up to what we deemed the best. My wife succeeded in this far more than I could, for she had a graciousness that I do not possess. It has always been my lot to have to struggle from one position to another. I used to describe my experience as comparable to a dive in a dirty swimming pool. When I begin the ascent, I open my eyes and I can scarcely see a thing. Then, as I rise things get lighter and lighter. In the actual pool, as a boy, I actually broke through the waterline and the great light burst on my eyes. In life, however, there is a change in the lightness, or an illusion thereof, but no bursting into the clear light.

Now I have talked to you as a father to a daughter. I hope that my side of the conversation will not trouble you. I can only understand that each must search for himself, and he has no alternative but to accept or turn away from that which he finds.

Love to all,
Carl E.W.L.Dahlstrom
[Letter to Rosalie (Sigler) Grafe]

Query: When religious instruction stands in the way of pursuit of personal wholeness, integrity, where do we take our questions?

JANUARY 16

John 11:32–36

32 Then when Mary was come where Jesus was, and saw him, she fell down at his feet, saying unto him, Lord, if thou hadst been here, my brother had not died.
33 When Jesus therefore saw her weeping, and the Jews also weeping which came with her, he groaned in the spirit, and was troubled.
34 And said, Where have ye laid him? They said unto him, Lord, come and see.
35 Jesus wept.
36 Then said the Jews, Behold how he loved him.

Goodness

Goodness, like morality, is individual, not social. To "leave a trace" goodness would have to enter the social arena.

CEWLD

Query: When we hear the groaning in the spirit of another, what are we moved to do?

JANUARY 17

Mark 3:33

33 And he answered them saying, Who is my mother, or my brethren?

Good Life, The

The good life for the Christian is oneness with God, wholeness. When fully comprehended, the good life is a total good life—no alienation, no estrangement. To be whole is to be free from all defect.

CEWLD

Query: If our children must leave us in search of the good life, of wholeness, how much of them do we release for the task and how far does our reach extend?

JANUARY 18

Isaiah 1:17

17 Learn to do well: seek judgment, relieve the oppressed, judge the fatherless, plead for the widow.

Do — What Shall We Do?

Vad att gora?
Quid facere?
Que faire?
Kya karun? (Gandhi said, 'What shall I do?')

CEWLD

Query: Do we send another back to the mercy of their cultural tradition and family based on the cultural and tradition and family of our own background? Will they be faithful to tell us of the fate that awaits them as a result of our kindness?

JANUARY 19

Psalm 84:3–4

3 Yea, the sparrow hath found an house, and the swallow a nest for herself, where she may lay her young, even thine altars, O LORD of hosts, my King and my God.
4 Blessed are they that dwell in thy house: they will be still praising thee. Selah.

Options

We are all born in a world of options. For some of us, the options are few; for others, the options are many. We rarely know what the options are when we are young: so if we are active, we often get slapped down. When we are old, we wonder whether life would have been better if we

had had precise knowledge of options. For those with fewest options—
would they just bow down to 'destiny'? And those with many options—
would they have the wisdom to choose the most rewarding options? And
what is finally 'most rewarding'?

CEWLD

Query: How do we prioritize our diminishing time to make wise use of
our options? How do we prioritize our options?

JANUARY 20

Hosea 2:23

23 And I will sow her unto me in the earth: and I will have mercy on her
that had not obtained mercy: and I will say unto them which were not my
people, Thou art my people: and they shall say, Thou art my God.

Bridewealth

Society recognizes the enormous domestic importance of women by
the institution of bridewealth, which not only guarantees the husband's
good behavior (in default of which his wife may leave him and he forfeits
the wealth) but which also places him in a subordinate position, for
the payment of wealth carries no absolute rights over the woman but
does carry heavy obligations. Above all, the wealth is a symbol of the
exchange that has taken place between two groups—not an exchange of
a woman for money, but an exchange of reciprocal obligations, duties and
responsibilities.

Colin M. Turnbull,
Man in Africa,
Garden City, NY, Anchor, 1976, p. 38

Query: "For this cause one leaves one's mother and father" (and people).
For what cause does one return to them? In what circumstance can one
remain a bridge between both?

JANUARY 21

Proverbs 2:2–4, 6–8

2 So that thou incline thine ear unto wisdom, and apply thine heart to understanding:

3 Yea, if thou criest after knowledge, and liftest up thy voice for understanding:

4 If thou seekest her as silver, and searchest for her as for hid treasures;

6. For the LORD giveth wisdom: out of his mouth cometh knowledge and understanding.

7. He layeth up sound wisdom for the righteous he is a buckler to them that walk uprightly.

8. He keepeth the paths of judgment, and preserveth the way of his saints.

Blindness (Non-physiological)

We read history. Repeatedly we are struck by the blindness of our predecessors. Why did they fail to see what we see so clearly—'as plain as the nose on your face'? This should give us pause.... Our predecessors were not aware of their blindness. Often enough they were snugly certain of positions taken (religious, moral, social, philosophical, scientific— whatever one can name). These 'blind' people assumed that they alone could see; everyone else was blind. And what about us? What incurable blindness attends our thoughts, speech and behavior? What are our irrational certainties and convictions? In what respects are we making it possible for our successors to exclaim, 'Why did they fail to see what we see so clearly—as plain as the nose on your face'?

CEWLD

Query: When faced with a crossroads, a pivotal decision, do we go with "gut instinct"? With our first impression? Or do we take the alternatives to season and study before rendering a decision? What roles do contemplation and prayer play in the process?

JANUARY 22

II Samuel 20:19

19 I am one of them that are peaceful and faithful in Israel: thou seekest to destroy a city and a mother in Israel; why wilt thou swallow up the inheritance of the LORD?

Birth

The Talmud says that every birth is a mistake, and that it would have been better for man not to be a part of creation. But because…yes, because, because he does live, he sanctifies life. Because he does work, he justifies his own plan. Because he does sing, he corrects the divine outline. Yes, because. Because all this IS, he says thank you. Because of it all, in spite of it all. Thank you, God. Thank you for having conferred these gifts, these faculties on me. This I can say: I, Moshe. Or else: You, God. You men: You, Death. Ultimately the self increases its powers, it does not let them erode. Thus I can speak while laughing, laugh while keeping silent, keep silent while screaming, live while dying and see myself without seeing.

Elie Wiesel,
The Oath, (1973),
New York, Avon, 1974, pp. 175–176

Query: How do we know that it is better that we are born?

JANUARY 23

Acts 17:16–21

16 Now while Paul waited for them at Athens, his spirit was stirred within him, when he saw the city wholly given to idolatry.
17 Therefore disputed he in the synagogue with the Jews, and with the devout persons, and in the market daily with them that met with him.
18 Then certain philosophers of the Epicureans, and the Stoicks encountered him. And some said, What will this babbler say? Other some, He seemeth to be a setter forth of strange gods because he preached unto them Jesus, and the resurrection.
19 And they took him, and brought him unto Aeropagus, saying: May we know what this new doctrine, which thou speakest, is?
20 For thou bringest certain strange things to our ear we would know therefore, what these things mean.
21 For all the Athenians and strangers that were there spent their time in nothing else, either to tell, or to hear some new thing.

Marginal Man

I am a marginal man. I was born and raised in a culture, once wholly steadfast and where life for a majority was almost fully predictable, and from which I have been uprooted. I live and work in a culture where change is desired because it is equated with progress, and where neither the physical nor the human scene is constant. The human being in whom two such contrasting cultures meet, moves, as it were, along the margin of each. He paces the border where they confront each other within himself, and he can reach out to touch them both. In that sense, this book is the report of a marginal man's life experience and his reflections upon it.

Francis L.K. Hsu,
Americans and Chinese,
Garden City, New York,
American Museum Science Books, 1972, p. xiii.

Query: The books of the Bible were largely the written down accounts by scribes of actions and stories of others. How much of the separate society of women was accurately written? How much is recorded of those coming from another culture and entering into the genealogies in scripture? Can we keep a foot in two worlds and speak for each?

JANUARY 24

Leviticus 20:26

26 And ye shall be holy unto me: for I the LORD am holy; and have severed you from other people, that ye should be mine.

Cultural Fusion

Even though modern research has shown that the individual comes into conflict with the group very early in primitive society, it is nevertheless certain that the further back we go in human history, the rarer individuality becomes and the more undeveloped it is. Indeed, even today, psychological analysis still comes up against the dead weight of collectively unconscious, non-individual factors in the psychology of modern man. From these two facts alone it must be sufficiently evident that man was originally part of the collective psyche of his group and enjoyed only the narrowest range of action as an individual. All the social, religious, and historical evidence points to the late birth of the individual from the collective and from the unconscious.

Erich Newmann,
The Origins and History of Consciousness,
Princeton, 1971, pp. 279–27

Query: How strongly can we stand alone? What happens when we take
our stand into a strange country?

JANUARY 25

Ephesians 2:19

19 Now therefore ye are no more strangers and foreigners, but fellow
citizens with the saints, and of the household of God.

Alienation

Modern society discourages fraternity and, as a result, those who become
discontented in its midst are most often alone. It is hard to sustain that
loneliness, much less to transform uneasiness and resentment into vision
and freedom. What is called "alienation" among us is, in fact, far removed
from the older meaning of the term. It does not refer to men who have
made themselves aliens because 'called out' by values higher than those of
the polity; they are citizens of a better city. Rather, it is usual to designate
those who are citizens nowhere. And the result is often a desperate
scrabbling to find affection and response somewhere, on almost any
terms—lost; finding his isolation unendurable, the individual falls into
conventionality, and respectability. Even 'nihilism' is often a request that
we bar the door; often we only open it wider, offering favor and adulation.
Unconventionality becomes first notoriety, then fashion, and finally a new
style of respectability. The real complaint against modern society is that in
so many ways it denies man the ability to become alienated.

Wilson Carey McWilliams,
The Idea of Fraternity in America (1973),
University of Colorado, 1974, p. 79.

Query: Are we more at peace in solitude or in the company of another or
others?

JANUARY 26

Proverbs 30:24–28 24

24 There be four [things which are] little upon the earth, but they [are] exceeding wise:
25 The ants [are] a people not strong, yet they prepare their meat in the summer;
26 The conies [are but] a feeble folk, yet make they make their houses in the rocks;
27 The locusts have no king, yet go they forth all of them by bands;
28 The spider taketh hold with her hands, and is in kings' palaces.

Significance

But there will also, I think, always be men and women who will transcend material existence. They will attain more and suffer more than others. But they will live significant lives. Perhaps this is only tinkling brass. But you can always be comforted by the feeling that you have elected to be a human being of good will and good faith. You have elected consciously to try to live up to your good will and good faith. I am convinced that it will support you and give you strength in the roles that you assume as well as those you take up voluntarily.

Letters to a Student: Correspondence and Reminiscences of Dr. Carl E.W.L. Dahlstrom, Rosalie V. Grafe, Ed.,
Quaker Abbey Press, LLC, 1999, p. 86

Query: Can we know the true significance of this moment?

JANUARY 27

Job 29:21–25

21 Unto me men gave ear, and waited, and kept silence at my counsel.
22 After my words they spake not again; and my speech dropped upon them.
23 And they waited for me as for the rain; and they opened their mouth wide as for the latter rain.
24 If I laughed on them, they believed it not; and the light of my

countenance they cast not down.
25 I chose out their way, and sat chief, and dwelt as a king in the army, as one that comforted the mourners.

Insider and Outsider

The Insider knows what the Outsider cannot know. The Outsider sees what the Insider cannot see.

Rev. Charles Riverdale [CEWLD]
Grandfather's Rocking Chair,
Privately published, 1971, p. 10

Query: How is influence earned and how is it carried over into a new community?

JANUARY 28

John 15:26–27

26 But when the Comforter is come, whom I will send unto you from the Father, even the Spirit of truth, which proceedeth from the Father, he shall testify of me;
27 And ye also shall bear witness because ye have been with me from the beginning.

Hymns, Concepts In

Again and again I wonder about the concepts in religious hymns. Do the people who sing them nowadays ever stop to think of what many of them imply? I am not thinking simply of the figures of reproach employed, [but of] all the implications in the language. Sometimes God is clearly an Oriental Despot. Repeatedly there is escapism—flight from this existence (and necessarily a condemnation of this existence). I suppose a study of hymns in the way I would suggest would constitute blasphemy for many of the believers. Yet they themselves do not understand how they twist and distort divinity until all the divinity is eliminated.

   Is this true: The convictions of the Religious Founder become the superstitions of his followers...?

CEWLD

Query: What do we think of when we read the hymn phrases "such a worm as I" and "despised not the Virgin's womb" and other questionable utterances? Do we sing them nevertheless? How does that feel?

JANUARY 29

Job 28:7–8

7 There was a path which no fowl knoweth, and which the vulture's eye hath never seen:
8 The lion's whelps have not trodden it, nor the fierce lion passed by it.

Optimism

Patently the way of the optimist is hard.

CEWLD

Query: The door of the lion, the door of the treasure, how to choose blindly?

JANUARY 30

Psalm 48:14

14 For this God is our God for ever and ever: he will be our guide, even unto death.

Respect

Respect for the dead signifies respect for the living—respect for the continuity of the human community and recognition of each man's place within it.

Eugene D. Genovese,
Roll Jordan Roll,
Pantheon Books, 1974, p. 202

Query: How do the ceremonies honoring the dead open new doors, new alliances?

JANUARY 31

II Kings 17:32–33

32 So they feared the LORD, and made unto themselves of the lowest of them priests of the high places which sacrificed for them in the houses of the high places.
33 They feared the LORD, and served their own gods, after the manner of the nations whom they carried away from thence.

Sectarianism

A sectarian can never be complete in his particular religion because the religion is always modified or quantified. He is not a full fledged believer in Islam, but a sectarian believer; not a full-fledged believer in Judaism but a sectarian believer; not a full fledged believer in Christianity, but a sectarian believer; so too with other religions.

CEWLD

Query: As we remember the admonition to not forsake gathering ourselves together (as believers) how do we identify the "selves" with whom we gather?

⌒FEBRUARY⌒

FEBRUARY 1

Ecclesiastes 3:1

1 To everything there is a season and a time for every purpose under the heaven:

Island of the Blessed

Only a few hints are to be found in Mesopotamian literature of any difference in the lot of the righteous and of the reprobate; thus we are told for example of the existence of an island of the blessed, to which a very small number of chosen ones were brought by the gods who first rendered them immortal.

Sabatino Moscate,
Ancient Semitic Civilizations (1957),
Cyericorn, 1976, p. 64

Query: Do we, to any extent, do good in anticipation of reward to come or do we do good to be in harmony with the Good?

FEBRUARY 2

Psalm 86:6

6 Give ear, O LORD, unto my prayer; and attend to the voice of my supplications.
7 In the day of my trouble I will call upon thee. O Lord; neither are there any works like thy works.

Pessimism

To the question whether I am a pessimist or an optimist, I answer that my knowledge is pessimistic... but my willing and hoping are optimistic.

I am pessimistic in that I experience in its full weight what we conceive to be the absence of purpose in the course of world happenings. Only at quite rare moments have I felt really glad to be alive. I could not but feel with a sympathy full of regret all the pain that I saw around me, not only that of men but that of the whole creation. From this community of suffering I have never tried to withdraw myself. It seemed to me a matter of course that we should all take our share of the burden of pain which lies upon the world. Even while I was a boy at school it was clear to me that no explanation of the evil in the world could ever satisfy me; all explanations, I felt, ended in sophistries, and at bottom had no other object than to make it possible for men to share in the misery around them with less keen feelings. That a thinker like Leibnitz could reach the miserable conclusion that though this world is, indeed, not good, it is the best that was possible, I have never been able to understand.

Albert Schweitzer,
Out of My Life and Thought (1933),
Mentor, 1955, p. 186

Query: Can we make it the "best of all possible worlds" for anyone? For ourselves? Or even that?

FEBRUARY 3

Romans 12:2

2 And be ye not conformed to this world: but be ye transformed by the renewing of your mind, that ye may prove what is good, and acceptable, and perfect, will of God.

Vulnerabilities

One of the reasons I can do what I do is that I've reduced my vulnerabilities.

Ralph Nader,
(Cited in *The New York Times*, Oct. 29, 1967, p. 111)

Query: How can we maintain our public reputation for integrity... preventatively...against allegations by antagonists?

FEBRUARY 4

John 1:11–14

11 These things have I spoken to you that my joy might remain in you, and that your joy might be full.
12 This is my commandment, That ye love one another, as I have loved you.
13 Greater love hath no man than this, that a man lay down his life for his friends.
14 Ye are my friends, if ye do whatsoever I command you.

Friends

Life is not worth living for the man who has not even one good friend.

Democritus of Abdera

What is a friend? Someone who for the first time makes you aware of your loneliness and his, and helps you to escape so you in turn can help him. Thanks to him you can hold your tongue without shame and talk freely without risk. That's it.

Elie Wiesel,
The Gates of the Forest, (1964),
Bard, Austin, TX, 1974, p. 37

But the good man is to his friend as to himself, friend being but a name for a second self....

Aristotle,
Nichomachean Ethics, IX, 117

Query: Are we truly vulnerable to our friends?

FEBRUARY 5

Joshua 1:9

9 Have not I commanded thee? Be strong and of a good courage; be not afraid, neither be thou dismayed: for the LORD thy God is with thee, whithersoever thou goest.

Fear

It is true that we cannot conquer death; we can, however, conquer our fear of death.

Nikos Kazantzakis,
Report to Greco,
New York, Simon and Schuster, 1965, p. 307

Query: What part of us is dismayed? What part walks the path ahead of the light? Of these, which is the faithful one? Both?

FEBRUARY 6

Romans 8:26–27

26 Likewise also the Spirit helpeth our infirmities for we know not what we should pray for as we ought: but the Spirit itself maketh intercession for us with groanings which cannot be uttered.
27 And he that searcheth the hearts knoweth what is the mind of the Spirit, because he maketh intercession for the saints according to the will of God.

Love

Love, the remaining summit of shared existence, is endangered by the growing belief that it can be separated from the commitment, which alone can sustain it.

Richard N. Goodwin,
The American Condition (1974),
N.Y., Bantam, 1975, p. 148

Query: The mystery of union, can we join it without having seen an example of its rewards in others?

FEBRUARY 7

Hebrews 6:12

12 ...followers of them who through faith and patience inherit the promises.

Disciple

The term 'disciple' is indicative of a form of education in which the student aligns him/herself with one teacher. For the most part, such alignment means subservience. The teacher is the Master; the disciple is the learner who tends to accept *in toto* the judgments and conclusions of the former....

CEWLD

Query: When one has outgrown the quest for a mentor, what are the signs? When one should accept a student, what are the signs?

FEBRUARY 8

Proverbs 17:17

17 A friend loveth for all times, and a brother is born for adversity.

Companion, The Good

If in a lifetime, one finds one person that never fails in goodness and love—parent, sibling, child, friend, mate, he is very fortunate. The good companion, the one who does not fail us, is as rare as Henry Adams friend:

'—one is much, two are many, and three well nigh impossible in one lifetime. (or words to that effect).'

CEWLD

Query: What do you fear in deeply befriending another person?

FEBRUARY 9

Psalm 119:19

19 I am a stranger in the earth: hide not thy commandments from me.

Discipline and Morality

Discipline = External Compulsion
Morality = Internal Conviction of the rightness of action

Discipline is the denial of option or, in the case of self-discipline, the creation of a force that functions as an external agent.

CEWLD

Query: What stops you?

FEBRUARY 10

I Corinthians 2:10–16

10 But God hath revealed them unto us by his Spirit: for the Spirit searcheth all things, yea, the deep things of God.
11 For what man knoweth the things of a man, save the spirit of man, which is in him? even so the things of God knoweth no man, but the Spirit of God.
12 Now we have received, not the spirit of the world but the Spirit which is of God; that we might know the things that are freely given to us of God.
13 Which things also we speak, not in the words which man's wisdom teacheth, but which the Holy Ghost teacheth; comparing spiritual things with spiritual.
14 But the natural man receiveth not the things of the Spirit of God: neither can he know them because they are spiritually discerned.
15 But he that is spiritual judgeth all things, yet he himself is judged of no man.
16 For who hath known the mind of the Lord, that he may instruct him? But we have the mind of Christ.

Saint and Saints

To take risks for a particular cause by providing sanctuary for its fugitives can be heroic, but to take risks on behalf of all fugitives, whoever they may be, and whatever the cause, is the prerogative of saints rather than of heroes.

Malcolm Muggeridge,
Chronicles of Wasted Time: Number 2,
"The Infernal,"
Grove (1973), Morrow, 1974, p. 248

Query: Our committed relationships, are they predetermined by God? Our marriages, children, parentage? If we believe this to be true, what changes? If not, then what?

FEBRUARY 11

Hebrews 13:1–3, 13–14, 18

1 Let brotherly love continue.
2 Be not forgetful to entertain strangers; for thereby some have entertained angels unawares.
3 Remember them that are in bonds, as bound with them; and them which suffer adversity, as being yourselves also in the body.
13 Let us go forth therefore unto him without the camp, bearing his reproach.
14 For here have we no continuing city, but we seek one to come.
18 Pray for us for we trust we have a good conscience, in all things willing to live honestly.

Love

Love, the remaining summit of shared existence, is endangered by the growing belief that it can be separated from the commitment which alone can sustain it.

Richard N. Goodwin,
The American Condition,
N.Y., Bantam, 1975, p. 148

Query: If "Love has gone" where did it go and can it come back?

FEBRUARY 12

Hebrews 3:14

14 For we are made partakers of Christ, if we hold the beginning of our confidence steadfast unto the end.

Stubborn

A stubborn person is one who insists on being his/her own person rather than what others say the he/she should be.

CEWLD

Query: What is the difference between: *steadfast, tenacious, stubborn* and— *faithful?*

FEBRUARY 13

Matthew 21:10–11

10 And when he was come into Jerusalem, all the city was moved saying, Who is this?
11 And the multitude said This is Jesus the prophet of Nazareth of Galilee.

Names

Now once a tribe member has a proper name, he can in a sense be recreated in his absence. 'He' can be thought about using 'thought' here in a special non-conscious sense of fitting into language structures.

Julian Jaynes,
The Origin of Consciousness in the Breakdown of the Bicameral Mind,
Boston, Houghton Mifflin, 1976, pp. 135–136

Query: If Ruth and Naomi (OT Book of Ruth) were refugees today, how and where would their story play out?

FEBRUARY 14

Judges 13:18

18 And the angel of the LORD said unto him, Why askesth thou thus after my name, seeing it is secret?

Names

When did names begin to lose their supernatural power?
When are they shortened or lengthened?
When did a name become little more than a pleasing sound?

CEWLD

Query: Do we alter our name to fit our new community's ability to pronounce or understand it? What does our name tell about us and our origins?

FEBRUARY 15

Ruth 1:2

2 And the name of the man was Elimelech [My God is King], and the name of his wife Naomi [Pleasant], and the name of his two sons Mahlon [Sick] and Chilion [Pining], Epaphrathites [city of Rachel's tomb on the Bethlehem road, Gen.35: 19] of Beth-lehem-Judah. [Bethlehem meant "House of Bread and Praise".]

The Holy Bible: Scofield Reference Edition,
King James Version (1909), C.I. Scofield, D.D. Ed.,
Oxford University Press, 1945, verse and references, p. 315

Names—2

In ancient times a man's name was a vital part of his being: the effacing of his name from his tomb destroyed his continued existence in the next world; the expunging of an official's name from the records ended that earthly success which was so important to his survival.

The Culture of Ancient Egypt (1951),
John A. Wilson,
University of Chicago Press, 1971, p. 225

Query: If you returned to your church of origin, what would be
remembered of your name and family?

FEBRUARY 16

Job 13:10–14

10 But he knoweth the way that I take; when he hath tried me I shall
come forth as gold.
11 My foot hath held his steps, his way have I kept, and not declined.
12 Neither have I gone back from the commandment of his lips; I have
esteemed the words of his mouth more than my necessary food.
13 But he is in one mind, and who can turn him? And what his soul
desireth, even that he doeth.
14 For he performeth the thing that is appointed for me: and many such
things are with him.

Failure in Social Change

We are at times bewildered by the failures of social reforms. Through the
5,000 years of recorded social events, there have been many changes; yet
the creation of a decent society of decent people has not been realized.
We forget two things; (1) social inertia, (2) people die. A society seems
to be able to change its ways only very slowly. In the United States, for
example, the slaves were freed in the 1860's; yet a century later, [1960's]
the majority of Blacks were treated as though they ought to be slaves
anyway! The law freed the Blacks; social inertia kept them in a situation
comparable to servitude.

   In the second place, people die. Those who enthusiastically worked for
change and got it on the lawbooks did not survive long enough to see the
change made effective in the ways of life. New generations spring up; they
have to learn anew and struggle anew.

   Social change occurs but not overnight. And it takes more than a new
law on the old books.

CEWLD

Query: How do we greet the stranger at our gate? At our border?

FEBRUARY 17

Psalm108:10–12

10 Who will bring me into the strong city? Who will lead me into Edom?
11 Wilt not thou, O God, go forth with our hosts?
12 Give us help from trouble; for vain is the help of man.

Deus Absconditas

Rebbe Baruth began to caress Yehiel's face and tears welled up in his eyes. 'God too, Yehiel,' he whispered softly, '...God too is unhappy; He is hiding and man is not looking for Him. Do you understand, Yehiel? God is hiding and man is not even searching for Him....'

Rebbe Barukh of Medzebozh,
Quoted by Elie Wiesel,
Four Hasidic Masters and their Struggle Against Melancholy,
University of Notre Dame Press, 1978, pp. 17 and 53

Query: Can we sense the sorrow of God? What then?

FEBRUARY 18

II Corinthians 12:25–27

25 ...a night and a day I have been in the deep.
26 In journeyings often, in perils of waters, in perils of robbers, in perils by mine own countrymen, in perils by the heathen, in perils in the city, in perils in the wilderness, in perils in the sea, in perils among false brethren;
27 In weariness and painfulness, in watchings often, in hunger and thirst, in fastings often, in cold and nakedness.

Morale and Fatalism

The American doughboys that I saw moving into action plodded along wearily, often with heads bowed. I never heard any of them singing. On one of my earliest encounters with such s column of infantrymen, I overheard one of my fellow tailgaters ask a weary marcher something about the 'battle for democracy.' The reply came out at once, a succinct, obscene imperative, an absolute dismissal of political ideals, notions of sacrifice, the justifiable war.

The doughboys were not fighting on the basis of ideologies; they were concentrating on the business of survival. They knew that every time they went into combat, the odds against survival were greatly increased. Some of them became superstitious. I heard one doughboy tell that he had been over the top twice, and had remained unscathed. But he was convinced that he would be killed in the engagement he was now entering. He was very depressed, haunted as he was by 'three times and out!' A few boasted, 'Nothing's got my number on it!' Fortunately for such fatalists and believers, no statistical studies had been made. They could thus retain their confidence that they would go through the entire war untouched....

Dr. Carl E.W. L. Dahlstrom,
1917–1919: a Personal History,
Portland, Oregon, 1980

Query: What keeps you from going forward?

FEBRUARY 19

Psalm 142

1 I cried unto the LORD with my voice; with my voice unto the LORD did I make my supplication.
2 I poured out my complaint before him; I shewed before him my trouble.
3 When my spirit was overwhelmed within me, then thou knewest my path. In the way wherein I walked have they privily laid a snare for me.
4 I looked on my right hand, and beheld, but there was no man that would know me: refuge failed me; no man cared for my soul.
5 I cried unto thee O LORD; I said, Thou art my refuge and my portion in the land of the living.
6 Attend unto my cry; for I am brought very low: deliver me from my persecutors; for they are stronger than I.
7 Bring my soul out of prison that I may praise thy name; the righteous shall compass me about; for thou shalt deal bountifully with me.

Failure

One can survive failure; it is much more difficult to survive success.

CEWLD

Query: When is failure only a stage?

FEBRUARY 20

Psalm 26:16–21

16 Turn thee unto me, and have mercy upon me; for I am desolate and afflicted.
17 The troubles of my heart are enlarged: O bring thou me out of my distresses.
18 Look upon mine affliction and my pain; and forgive all my sins.
19 Consider mine enemies; for they are many; and they hate me with cruel hatred.
20 O keep my soul, and deliver me: let me not be ashamed; for I put my trust in thee.
21 Let integrity and uprightness preserve me; for I wait on thee.

Desert Recluses

Sometimes we wonder about those persons who isolated themselves in the deserts. Were they sheer escapists, fleeing the diurnal realities of human existence? Were they genuinely religious, seeking to become one with the spiritual force(s)? Or was it impossible in many societies to have a thought of one's own unless he or she could isolate him/herself from the din and order and duties of diurnal existence?

The fearful contradiction comes to mind: (a) to be fully oneself, and (b) to be fully responsive to society. Most men and women are unable to fulfill themselves socially and individually, hence they commonly let one or the other be the determining force.

CEWLD

Query: What precedes a longing for solitude?

FEBRUARY 21

Psalm 4:2–4

2 O ye sons of men, how long will ye turn my glory into shame? How
long will ye love vanity…?
3 But know that the LORD hath set apart him that is godly for himself:
the LORD will hear when I call unto him.
4 Stand in awe, and sin not: commune with your own heart upon your
bed, and be still. Selah.

Desiderata

What do people want? If we judge from TV, radio, tapes, records,
theatre, books, news media, entertainment, sports and general 'leisure
time activities,' we should conclude that what is desired is a confusion of
violence and sentiment, deceptive ad facts, activity and changelessness, all
qualified somehow by sex. The judgment is based on the assumption that
people really know what they want. But do they?

A great part of growing up, of attaining maturity, is determining
personal values. Not knowing what they want, the majority of people tend
to accept what they get. Perhaps many gradually come to believe that they
want what they get.

Note that this confusion arises largely in individual-oriented societies.
In group-centered societies the attempt is made so to condition people
that they believe they want what they get. The attempt is never completely
successful….

CEWLD

Query: What would "world peace" look like?

FEBRUARY 22

I Corinthians 15:51–2

51 Behold, I shew you a mystery: We shall not all sleep, but we shall all be
changed.
52 In a moment, in the twinkling of an eye….

Change and Chance

The world in which we are set is a world of change and chance in which nothing is ever perfected, nothing permanent, nothing secure. But the world can be understood: through the change of this world we can come to know truths.... The world as we experience it may be held to exist for the sake of leading minds to words. What is 'permanent', 'changeless' and 'perfect' in itself?

Karl Britton,
Philosophy and the Meaning of Life,
Cambridge University Press, 1969, p. 52

Query: Why do we defend ourselves even against advantageous change? What happens when we let go of the edge of the swimming pool and plunge ahead?

FEBRUARY 23

Nehemiah 2:5–7

5 And I said unto the king, If it please the king, and if thy servant have found favour in thy sight, that thou wouldest send me into Judah, unto the city of my fathers' sepulchers, that I may build it.
6 And the king said unto me, (the queen also sitting by him) For how long shall thy journey be? And when wilt thou return? So it pleased the king to send me; and I set him a time.
7 Moreover I said unto the king, If it please the king, let letters be given me to the governors beyond the river that they may convey me over till I come unto Judah;

Life

The Gift of Life is always balanced by the Sentence of Death.

CEWLD

Query: George Eliot's question: *Is it ever too late to become what we might have been?*

FEBRUARY 24

Luke 18:31–34

31 Then he took unto him the twelve, and said unto them, Behold, we go up to Jerusalem, and all things that are written by the prophets concerning the Son of man shall be accomplished.

31 For he shall be delivered unto the Gentiles, and shall be mocked, and spitefully entreated, and spitted on.

33 And they shall scourge him and put him to death: and the third day he shall rise again.

34 And they understood none of these things, this saying was hid from them, neither knew they the things which were spoken.

Life and Death

'There came upon me,' replied he, ' a sudden pity, when I thought of the shortness of man's life, and considered that of all this host, so numerous as it is, not one will be alive when a hundred years are gone by.'

'And yet there are sadder things in life than that,' returned the other, 'Short as our time is, there is no man, whether he be here among this multitude or elsewhere, who is so happy as not to have felt the wish—I will not say once, but full many a time—that he were dead rather than alive. Calamities fall upon us; sicknesses vex and harass us, and make life, short though it be, to appear long. So death, through the wretchedness of our life, is a most sweet refuge to our race: and God, who gives us the tastes that we enjoy of pleasant times is seen, in his very gift, to be envious.'

The History of Herodotus,
Tr. Geo. Rawlinson,
New York, Dutton, 1910, Vol. 11, p. 139

Query: Would you live beyond the span of those you love?

FEBRUARY 25

Joel 2:12–13

12 Therefore also now saith the LORD, turn ye even to me with all your heart, and with fasting, and with weeping, and with mourning.

13 And rend your heart, and not your garments, and turn unto the LORD your God; for he is gracious and merciful, slow to anger, and of great kindness, and repenteth him of the evil.

Rest of Us, The

The rest of us, the deprived, the have-nots, the disinherited, the last on every list including God's, have we no cause to fear? Who would be stupid enough to covet our fate?

Elie Wiesel,
The Oath (1973),
New York, Avon, 1974, p. 204

Query: Can we ever be secure by not arousing envy? Can we humble ourselves to invisibility? Does God want this?

FEBRUARY 26

Luke 22:52–53

52 Then Jesus said unto the chief priests, and captains of the temple, and the elders, which were come unto him, Be ye come out, as against a thief, with swords and staves?
53 When I was daily with you in the temple, ye stretched forth no hands against me: but this is your hour, and the power of darkness.

The Politics of Death

There was very little popular enthusiasm in Massachusetts Bay for the death penalty against Quakers, but it was enacted in 1658, having passed the House of Deputies by a majority of only one vote.

Daniel J. Boorstin,
The Americans: The Colonial Experience,
New York, Vintage, 1958, p. 38

Query: Who defines Enemy for us? Does this change our faith-obligation?

FEBRUARY 27

Psalm 3:5

5 I laid me down and slept, I awaked; for the LORD sustained me.
Suffering

'Zeus, who prepared for man the path of wisdom, binding fast learning to
suffering.'

Aeschylus,
Agamemnon, Translated by Lewis Campbell,
The World's Classics: Aeschylus: Seven Plays in English Verse
Oxford University Press, 1949, Lines 175–177

It may be true, as Aeschylus says, that we learn through suffering. This
does not mean, however, that we are eager and happy pupils. Some people
can relieve their suffering solely by making everyone around them suffer.
In this case, *misery demands company.*

Query: Is there ever a day when we are unable to laugh?

FEBRUARY 28

Joel 2:12–13

12 Therefore also now saith the LORD, turn ye even to me with all your
heart, and with fasting, and with weeping, and with mourning.
13 And rend your heart, and not your garments, and turn unto the LORD
your God; for he is gracious and merciful, slow to anger, and of great
kindness, and repenteth him of the evil.

Seeing

As we learn from our immediate experiences and from our readings, much
in human existence is illusion and delusion, and there are no guaranteed
means of acquiring total vision. I rub my eyes and look, and then rub
them again and take another look. The way that I see things is the way
that I now seem to see them with whatever quality of vision I possess.
But I am trying to see.

CEWLD

Query: When we do see, then what?

FEBRUARY 29

Luke 9:62

62 And Jesus said unto him, No man, having put his hand to the plough and looking back is fit for the kingdom of God.

Perspective

A cat may look at a king, and the latter may be unaffected thereby in all his kingly functions. But it is of the essence of his reality (or of the world of which he is a part) that he should present the specific view, which, in the cat's perspective, he does.

Morris R. Cohen,
Reason and Nature: an Essay on the Meaning of Scientific Method
New York, Harcourt, Brace and Company, 1931, p. 239

Query: When we close the door on the past, what changes?

⇜MARCH⇝

MARCH 1

Proverbs 31:30–31

30 Favour is deceitful and beauty is vain: but a woman that feareth the LORD, she shall be praised.
31 Give her of the fruit of her hands; and let her own works praise her in the gates.

Women

In a patriarchal society, woman had significance only if:

(1) she was the daughter of a significant man,
(2) the wife of a significant man,

(3) the mother of a significant man,
(4) was a queen,
(5) became an outstanding criminal.

CEWLD

Query: Ruth had eyes to see and boldness to take a direction, in other words, Courage. Do you see an opportunity in this day?

MARCH 2

Genesis 32:26

26 And he said, Let me go, for the day breaketh, And he said, I will not let thee go, except thou bless me.

Women

All men, in the end, make impossible demands on women....

John Wain,
Samuel Johnson,
New York, Viking, 1974, p. 269

Twentieth century woman has gained more independence than the sex has ever enjoyed. The price has been greatly increased insecurity. In other words, present-day woman is less independent than the male but far more insecure than he is.

CEWLD

Query: As independent women, could Ruth of Moab and Naomi of Bethlehem have made the same choices if there were small children involved? What if they did?

MARCH 3

Isaiah 54:1

1 Sing, O barren, thou that didst not bear: break forth into singing, and

cry aloud, thou that didst not travail with child: for more are the children of the desolate than the children of the married wife, saith the LORD.

Social Discontinuity

A society that is going through a process of dislocation and upheaval, or of revolution, is bound to cause suffering to individuals, but this suffering itself can bring one closer to one's own existence. Habit and routine are great veils over our existence. As long as they are securely in place, we need not consider what life means; its meaning seems sufficiently incarnate in the triumph of the daily habit. When the social fabric is rent, however, man is suddenly thrust outside, away from the habits and norms he once accepted automatically. There, on the outside, his questioning begins.

William Barrett,
Irrational Man, A Study in Existential Philosophy,
Anchor/Doubleday, 1962, p. 135

Query: The adjustment to a new home, a new job, a new land, how long does it take?

MARCH 4

Proverbs 10:15

15 The rich man's wealth is his strong city: the destruction of the poor is their poverty.

Suffering (to minimize)

How can we minimize suffering for ourselves?

One way is to live in the fullness of the Continuum of Occurrence. To be able to do this, one must also live in the fullness of himself. It is through the sympathetic and empathetic relationship of the two fullnesses that one can reduce suffering to a minimum.

1. You have to be yourself, your own person—nobody's man, no organization's man.
2. That self has to feel itself into (*Einfuhlung*) the fullness of the

Continuum of Occurrence.
3. The suffering is not totally eliminated, but it is controlled and reduced to a minimum.

CEWLD

Query: What are the differences between voluntary simplicity, subsistence and bare bones survival?

MARCH 5

Psalm 18:18–22

18 They prevented me in the day of my calamity; but the LORD was my stay.
19 He brought me forth also into a large place; he delivered me, because he delighted in me.
20 The LORD rewarded me according to my righteousness; according to the cleanness of my hands hath he recompensed me.
21 For I have kept the ways of the LORD, and have not wickedly departed from my God.
22 For all his judgments were before me, and I did not put away his statutes from me.

To Live in Your Perception

The stars cast no shadow.
Knife turning in wound,
It is decided.

From Royal David's City,
From Nazareth's alley,
The desert's grinding wind,
Galilee's blinding shore,
He comes.

Diminishment, distillation,
Down-driven, homeless yet home,
Less, and yet much more.

All of Heaven's glory,

Inside a homespun cloak,
Inside a skin of skin,
Vulnerable to nails.

The King of Glory,
Shrunk to our feeble,
Field of vision,
Hung on high for
Ridicule and adoration
Together.

Taken down,
In that skin of skin,
And rising undiminished,
Infinite yet capable,
Of sinking into the very heart
Of faith.

R.V. Grafe,
Lenten Meditations from All Saints Episcopal Church,
All Saints Episcopal Church, 2000

Question: When at the crossroads, do we look up or do we seek within?

MARCH 6

Deuteronomy 10:18–19

18 He doth execute the judgment of the fatherless and widow, and loveth
the stranger, in giving him food and raiment.
19 Love ye therefore the stranger for ye were strangers in the land of
Egypt.

Wealth

Wealth, under primitive conditions, consists in the supply of corn
upon which man must exist during the season of the year when Nature
produces nothing. He, who has nothing, must starve.

Martin P. Nilsson,
A History of Greek Religion (1925) 2nd Ed. rev. (1952)

New York, Norton, 1964, pp. 122–123

Query: What is our attitude toward those who take government assistance and what would it take for us to do so?

MARCH 7

Psalm 69:15–17

15 Let not the waterflood overflow me, neither let the deep swallow me up and let not the pit shut her mouth upon me.
16 Hear me, O LORD; for thy lovingkindness is good; turn unto me according to the multitude of thy tender mercies.
17 And hide not thy face from thy servant; for I am in trouble: hear me speedily.

Wealth

In Sicily the festival of harvest was … called 'the bringing down of the [corn-] maiden', i.e. into the underground storehouse. Down there she was in the power of Pluto the subterranean god of wealth, until at the sowing she was again brought up and united to her mother Demeter, the goddess of agriculture.

Martin P. Nilsson,
A History of Greek Religion (1925), 2nd Ed., rev. (1952),
New York, Norton,1964, pp. 122-123

Query: When we look within for our own buried treasure, what talents can we nourish back to bloom under the challenge to survival needs? (See *The Dollmaker*, Harriet Simpson Arnow. Macmillan, 1958)

MARCH 8

II Corinthians 9:8–10

8 And God is able to make all grace abound toward you; that ye always having all sufficiency in all things, may abound to every good work:
9 As it is written, He hath dispersed abroad; he hath given to the poor: his righteousness remaineth forever.

10 Now he that ministereth seed to the sower both minister bread for your food, and multiply your seed sown, and increase the fruits of your righteousness.

Prosperity

What is bad? Too much? Too little? Moreover, the balance between the two is never attained with justice to all.

CEWLD

Query: Who among us has the faith to face the dawn with nothing—but faith— to fill the day?

MARCH 9

Psalm 37:23

23 The steps of a good man are ordered by the LORD: and he delighteth in his way.

Career

The greatest career that anyone can possibly have is that of a decent human being.

CEWLD

Utterances, Mutterances and Sputterances from Grandfather's Rocking Chair: Selected, Compiled, Bowdlerized and Edited by 'The Rev. Charles M. Riverdale, Jr.' [CEWLD], Privately published for friends, 1978

Query: What prevents us from what we ought to do?

MARCH 10

Proverbs 27:21

21 As a fining pot for silver, and the furnace for gold; so is a man to his praise. Praise

What's this? No one says nice things about you? No one compliments you? No one makes you feel good about yourself?

Well, get to work! Just make a tape recording of all the nice things you'd like to hear. If you are affluent, you can hire it done (as though for someone else of course). But your own voice will sound different from your voice as you hear it naturally; so go ahead, make your tapes! Listen! Blush with pleasure.

You might even go into business making 'personality tapes' for others!

N.B. If by chance you are a masochist, here is your chance to deliver to yourself all the monstrous blows you have dreamed of. Hurry up! Enjoy yourself!

CEWLD

Query: When we bless others, praise others, do we require the same in return...or no return but the warmth given by the giving.

MARCH 11

Acts 4:25

25 Ye are the children of the prophets, and of the covenant which God made with our fathers, saying unto Abraham, And in thy seed shall all the kindreds of the earth be blessed.

Kindness

To remind a man of kindness conferred, and to talk of it, is little different from reproach.

Samuel Johnson

Query: Do we do our kindness in secret and without a tax deduction?

MARCH 12

Proverbs 31:31

31 Give her of the fruit of her hands; and let her own works praise her in the gates.

Kindness—2

It is difficult to be kind to people who do not want you to be kind—only inferior. They tend to look upon you as an easy mark; they act as though you have deceived them! I have encountered such people chiefly on the faculties of universities, both those that call themselves great and those that are more modest.

CEWLD

Query: Do we do our kindness with an expectation of response…or not?

MARCH 13

Micah 5:2

2 But thou, Bethlehem Ephratah, though thou be little among the thousands of Judah, yet out of thee shall come forth unto me he that is to be ruler in Israel; whose goings forth have been from of old, from everlasting.

Matthew 2:1–2

1 Now when Jesus was born in Bethlehem of Judea in the days of Herod the king, behold, there came wise men from the east to Jerusalem.
2 Saying, Where is he that is born King of the Jews? For we have seen his star in the east, and are come to worship him.

Prophet

Successful prophets are the great artists in the transformation of their gods.

A. Eustace Haydon
Biography of the Gods,
New York, Macmillan, 1941, p. 20

The prophets were the creative thinkers of their day, the sources of wisdom. Those who organized religions out of the utterances of the prophets were the imitative thinkers, the sources of social stasis. The former brought new life to the world; the latter changed the new life into dead forms. The prophet is always in quest of the dynamic, the vibrating, the living, that which is ever bursting into newness, that which glows. The organizer is concerned with order, plant efficiency, the unchanging, and ultimately that which is dead.

CEWLD

Query: Do we try to re-hear, re-see the eternal stories in light of our own transitory significance?

MARCH 14

Isaiah 35:1

1 The wilderness and the solitary place shall be glad for them: and the desert shall rejoice and blossom as the rose.

Prophet—2

A prophet is a man who has been dead a long, long time. You don't have to stone him anymore.

CEWLD

Query: If we cannot hear the voices of the prophets, can we hear the stones that cry out, the hills that clap their hands for joy, the voice in the whirlwind or in the stillness?

MARCH 15

Proverbs 6:6–8

6 Go to the ant thou sluggard; consider her ways and be wise:
7 Which having no guide, overseer or ruler,
8 Provideth her meat in the summer, and gathereth her meat in the harvest.

Prophet—3

The great prophets—from the ancient Jews to the ghost-dance Paiute leaders and Melanesian millenarians of more recent time—were outsiders who often, like Muhammad, had to leave home to gain a following among strangers. Normally they preached to hostile audiences. Even in the Christian era with the organized communities of the faithful, the prophet appears as an individual agent of challenge to the religious and secular order. In proclaiming a new law, even in the guise of a return to an older interpretation of existing law 'It is written...but I say unto you...' the prophet assumes the role of a revolutionary leader.

Eugene D. Genovese,
Roll Jordan Roll,
New York, Pantheon, 1972, 1974, p. 278

Query: Ruth was the great grandmother of King David. Was she a prophet according to the qualifications set forth in today's quote...or some other way?

MARCH 16

Ephesians 6:5–9

5 Servants, be obedient to them that are your masters according to the flesh, with fear and trembling in singleness of your heart, as unto Christ.
6 Not with eyeservice as menpleasers; but as the servants of Christ, doing the will of God from the heart;
7 With good will doing service, as to the Lord, and not to men;
8 Knowing that whatsoever good thing any man doeth, the same shall he receive of the Lord, whether he be bond or free.
9 And ye masters, do the same things unto them, forbearing threatening: knowing that your Master also is in heaven; neither is there respect of persons with him.

Prophets

Prophets lead the way, but the followers can never keep up with them. So the latter catch onto a phrase, a concept, a gesture and out of that they build a common life. Meanwhile the prophet goes his lonely way, wondering whether his version is madness, unable to talk to anyone with receptive understanding.

'There was a great light!' cries the prophet.

'I know, I know!' answers the follower.

'The moon was very bright last night. Time for planting.'

CEWLD

Query: Have we ever been "the prophet" and could we recognize our own words for that kind of instruction for ourselves?

MARCH 17

Galatians 6:9

9 And let us not be weary in well doing; for in due season we shall reap, if we faint not.

Will (the) and Unity

Determinists and indeterminists speak of intellect, will, the body, the emotions, and the like as though a human being were something like a rag bag containing a variety of independent elements held together only because in the same bag.

In physics we are acquainted with the phenomenon that at one time is best interpreted as a wave and at another time as a particle. It is the same phenomenon—it is not two items acting out of one bag. The same holds true of will, intellect and the like. It is not the WILL speaking as though it were a person within a person; it is the person in entirety. One person does not pick up a tool, a second talk, and a third whistle—it is the same person. Unless we have the unusual phenomenon of Dr. Jekyll and Mr. Hyde, we have a unified human field of action. It is no more absurd to speak of will than of the different facets of any item or the different aspects [of the whole person].

CEWLD

Query: What keeps us on past the point of weariness and with no end in sight?

MARCH 18

Psalm 119:49–50

49 Remember the word unto thy servant, upon which thou hast caused me to hope.
50 This is my comfort in my affliction: for thy word hath quickened me.

Reverence for Life

Affirmation of life is the spiritual act by which man ceases to live unreflectively and begins to devote his life reflectively and with reverence in order to raise it to its true value. To affirm life is to deepen, to make more inward, and to exalt the will-to-live.

Albert Schweitzer,
Out of My Life and Thought: An Autobiography,
Tr. C.T. Campion (1933),
New York, Mentor, 1955, p.126

Query: Do fatigue and the heat of the day mar our reverence for life, our ability to listen inwardly?

MARCH 19

Philemon Verse 21

21 Having confidence in thy obedience I wrote unto thee knowing that thou wilt also do more than I say.

Doing and Undoing

The reason why we are never able to foretell with certainty the outcome and end of any action is simply that--action has no end.
     The process of a single deed can quite literally endure throughout time until mankind itself has come to an end.
     That deeds possess such an enormous capacity for endurance, superior to every other man-made product, could be a matter of pride if men were able to bear its burden, the burden of irreversibility and unpredictability,

from which the action process draws its very strength. That this is impossible, men have always known. They have known that he who acts never quite knows what he is doing, that he always becomes 'guilty' of consequences he never intended or even foresaw, that no matter how disastrous and unexpected the consequences of his deed [or how glorious] he can never undo it, that the process he starts is never consummated unequivocally in one single deed or event and that its very meaning never discloses itself to the actor but only to the backward glance of the historian who himself does not act. All this is reason enough to turn away with despair from the realm of human affairs and to hold in contempt the human capacity for freedom which by producing the web of human relationships, seems to entangle its producers to such an extent that he appears much more the victim and the sufferer than the author and doer of what he has done. Nowhere, in other words, neither in labor, subject to the necessity of life, nor in fabrication, dependent upon given material, does man appear to be less free than in those capacities whose very essence is freedom and with that realm which owes its existence to nobody and nothing but man.

It is in accordance with the great tradition of Western thought to think along these line to accuse freedom of wiring man into necessity, to condemn action, the spontaneous beginning of something new, because its results fall into a predetermined net of relationships, invariably dragging the agent with them who seems to forfeit his freedom the very moment he makes use of it.

Hanna Arendt
The Human Condition (1958),
University of Chicago, 1974, pp. 233–234

Query: As Boaz' charity to Ruth changed the future of Israel and put him in the ancestral line of Christ, what consequences have we unleashed by deep involvement in the lives of individuals and community?

MARCH 20

John 4:6–15, 19–25

6 Now Jacob's well was there. Jesus therefore, being wearied with his journey, sat thus on the wall: and it was about the sixth hour.
7 There cometh a woman of Samaria to draw water: Jesus saith unto her, Give me to drink.

8 (For his disciples were gone over unto the city to buy meat.)
9 Then saith the woman of Samaria unto him, How is it that thou, being a Jew, asketh drink of me, which am a woman of Samaria? For the Jews have no dealings with the Samaritans.
10 Jesus answered and said unto her, If thou knowest the gift of God, and who it is that saith to thee, Give me to drink; thou wouldest have asked of him, and he would have given thee living water.
11 The woman saith unto him, Sir, thou hast nothing to draw with, and the well is deep: from whence then hast thou that living water?
12 Art thou greater than our father Jacob, which gave us the well and drank thereof himself and his children and his cattle?
13 Jesus answered and said unto her; Whosoever drinketh of this water shall thirst again:
14 But whosoever drinketh of the water that I shall give him shall never thirst; but the water that I give him shall be in him shall be in him a well of water springing up into everlasting life.
15 The woman saith unto him, Sir, give me this water, that I thirst not, neither come hither to draw.
19 The woman saith unto him, Sir, I perceive that thou art a prophet.
20 Our fathers worshipped in this mountain; and ye say that in Jerusalem is the place where men ought to worship.
21 Jesus saith unto her, Woman, believe me, the hour cometh, when ye shall, neither in this mountain, nor yet in Jerusalem, worship the Father.
22 Ye worship ye know not what: we know what we worship: for salvation is of [to come from] the Jews.
23 But the hour cometh and now is when the true worshippers shall worship the Father in spirit and in truth; for the Father seeketh such to worship him.
24 God is a Spirit and they that worship him must worship him in spirit and in truth.
25 The woman saith unto him, I know that Messias cometh, which is called Christ: when he is come he will tell us all things.
26 Jesus saith unto her, I that speak to thee am he.

Merit

In harmony with a Shakespearean dictum, we do not treat people according to their merits. We treat them according to their need.

CEWLD

Query: How do we determine the need of another and our resources to assist?

MARCH 21

I Peter: 5–7

5 Likewise, ye younger, submit yourselves unto the elder. Yea, all of you be subject one to another, and be clothed with humility: for God resisteth the proud, and giveth grace to the humble.
6 Humble yourselves therefore under the mighty hand of God, that he may exalt you in due time;
7 Casting all your cares upon him: for he careth for you.

God-Man

Christ's Passion was not much dwelt upon in Eastern Christendom. What counted there was his Transfiguration; Christ was the Lord of the Cosmos; He was caught up as man into the circle of light radiating from the 'triple sun of the Godhead, which shed on man its benignant radiance' this was the teaching about the humanity of Christ current in the Eastern Church.

But God became man, and wholly man, born a naked infant and laid in the manger. Francis set up his Crib at Greccio not as a pretty toy but to be a dread and solemn warning to the mighty, the theologians and to ordinary Christian 'Behold your God, a poor and helpless child, the ox and the ass beside Him.' (Walther von der Vogelweide had uttered the same admonition.) 'Your God is of your flesh, he lives in your nearest neighbor, in every man, for all men are your brothers.'

Frederick Heer,
The Medieval World (Mittelalter), 1961 tr. English 1962
New York, Mentor, n.d., p. 223

Query: If fate turns us into helpless dependents, can we wait in faith for grace?

MARCH 22

Psalm 90:16–17

16 Let thy work appear unto thy servants, and thy glory unto their children.

17 And let the beauty of the Lord our God be upon us; and establish thou the work of our hands upon us; yea the work of our hands establish thou it.

God's Name

'Father, what name do you give God?' asked the abbe.

'God does not have a name,' the dervish replied.
'He is too big to fit inside names. A name is a prison, God is free.'

Nikos Kazantzakis,
Report to Greco,
New York, Simon and Schuster, 1965, p. 152

Eckhart says 'God is inexpressible and he has no name. At bottom the soul is also inexpressible as He is.' The Bhagavad Gita says the same.

Rudolf Otto,
Mysticism East and West,
New York, Macmillan, 1970, p. 99, footnote 2

Query: Is the success of our work in its effectiveness or in the reward we receive for it? Must that reward be outwardly visible?

MARCH 23

Lamentations 4:9

9 They that be slain with the sword are better than they that be slain with hunger: for these pine away, stricken through for want of the fruits of the field.

Matthew 25:37–40

37 Then shall the righteous answer him, saying, Lord, when saw we thee an hungred and fed thee? or thirsty, and gave thee drink?
38 When saw we thee a stranger, and took thee in? or naked and clothed thee?
39 Or when saw we thee sick, or in prison, and came unto thee?

40 And the King shall answer and say unto them, Verily I say unto you, Inasmuch as ye have done it unto one of the least of these my brethren, ye have done it unto me.

Food (Malnutrition of World's Children)

WASHINGTON, Oct. 5, (1974)—In parts of rural Bangladesh, during relatively good times, villagers hope to eat one meal a day. This year, during the aftermath of the summer floods, many of them were eating only once every other day, sometimes only once in every three.

An authority on world malnutrition, Dr. Nevin S. Scrimshaw, cited these grim figures recently to put in human terms the impact of hunger in 1974.

The consequence of prolonged hunger is malnutrition. It is widespread in the underdeveloped world. It appears to be getting worse. It hits children hardest, killing many and stunting the growth of many others both mentally and physically so that they are likely to be handicapped for life.

Since early this year, nutritionists say, there have been sharp increases in serious malnutrition among young children in many regions, notably Barbados, Guatemala, Bangladesh, Thailand and India.

There are no good global figures on malnutrition and never have been, but some experts estimate that a billion or more people suffer from it during at least part of the year. That means that almost a third of the human race are suffering today from hunger and its consequences.

Malnutrition and its ultimate form—starvation—are the real causes of world concern over the teetering balance between the food supplies and population across the globe....

Nations that appear to be particularly hard hit include India, Pakistan, Bangladesh, the sub-Saharan countries of Africa, Indonesia and parts of several Latin-American countries.

It has been estimated that roughly 15 million children a year die before the age of 5 of the combined effects of infection and malnutrition. This annual toll represents a quarter of all the deaths in the world [and much more].

Harold M. Schmeck Jr.,
"Malnutrition Is Up Sharply Among World's Children,"
The New York Times, Sunday, October 6, 1974 Section One, p. 1.

Query: Why is the malnutrition and disease of the world's children no longer news? What global concerns replaced it?

MARCH 24

Philemon, Verses 15–16

15 For perhaps he therefore departed for a season, that thou shoudest receive him for ever;
16 Not now as a servant, but above a servant, a brother beloved, specially to me, but now much more unto thee, both in the flesh and in the Lord?

Morality Defined [As a Frame of Reference]

1. Harmlessness—akin to the *Ahimsa* of India
2. Forbearance—control such that one can absorb insolence, insults, and even injury without resorting to violence. (This does not necessarily mean total acceptance of all violence attempted upon one.)
3. Fairness—a powerful sense of individual and social justice.
4. Disinterested Benevolence (term borrowed from Samuel Hopkins, 1721-1803)— A person performs acts of human decency because the situation seems to require them, but there is neither expectation nor acceptance of honor or profit.
5. Candor-Openness-Integrity— A moral person is one, is whole, not an active mixture of rogue and saint, or the like. Not 'all things to all people' but one and the same. Morality is not a form of salesmanship or propaganda.

I [CEWLD] prefer 'harmlessness' to 'nonviolence,' because it, at least on the surface, is more inclusive. Nonviolence conjures up a picture of mayhem, arson, ...and the like. Harmlessness, however, requires the inviolability not only of the body but also of the mind. One does no harm that is physiological, psychological, or social; in truth, one perpetrates no harm of any kind. 'Harmlessness' of course, is an ideal to be approached rather than attained. For it is highly doubtful if anyone can go through life without at least accidentally harming others or even doing so in a form of self-defense. After all, there is none good but one—God! (Mark 10:18)

CEWLD

Query: By doing no harm, do we delegate our "harming" to others by default?

MARCH 25

I Peter 2:19–20

19 For this is thankworthy, if a man for conscience toward God endure grief, suffering wrongfully,
20 For what glory is it, if when ye be buffeted for your faults ye shall take it patiently? but if, when ye do well, and suffer for it, ye take it patiently, this is acceptable with God.

Moral Life

Nothing erodes the public morality as much as the acquiescence in what is expedient when what is true is unpalatable.

J. Bronowski,
The Identity of Man, Revised Edition,
Garden City, N.Y.,
Museum Science Books Edition, 1971, p. 110

Query: When do we say "Here I stand; I can do no other"?

MARCH 26

Luke 7:4–10

4 And when they came to Jesus, they besought him instantly, saying that he was worthy for whom he should do this
5 For he loveth our nation, and he hath built us a synagogue.
6 Then Jesus went with them. And when he was now not far from the house, the centurion sent friends to him saying unto him, Lord, trouble not thyself; for I am not worthy that thou shouldest enter under my roof:
7 Wherefore neither thought I myself worthy to come unto thee: but say in a word, and my servant shall be healed.
8 For I also am a man set under authority, having under me soldiers and I say unto one, Go, and he goeth; and to another, Come, and he cometh; and to my servant, Do this, and he doeth it.
9 When Jesus heard these things, he marveled at him, and turned him about, and said unto the people that followed him, I say unto you, I have

not found so great faith, no not in Israel.

10 And they that were sent, returning to the house, found the servant whole that had been sick.

Honor

If a person's work honors him (her), the honor of his (her) fellow human beings is superfluous. If a person's work does not honor him (her), then the honor of his (her) fellow human beings is without foundation.

CEWLD

Query: Can our lives honor God?

MARCH 27

Proverbs 3:1–6

1 My son, forget not my law; but let thine heart keep my commandment
2 For length of days, and long life, and peace, shall they add to thee.
3 Let not mercy and truth forsake thee; bind them about thy neck; write them upon the table of thine heart:
4 So shalt thou find favour and good understanding in the sight of God and man.
5 Trust in the LORD with all thine heart: and lean not to thine own understanding.
6 In all thy ways acknowledge him, and he shall direct thy paths.

Blessings and Handicaps

Each one of our lives is elevated by the blessings of the age into which we are thrust. Each one is depressed by the handicaps. Happy are those who have been more elevated than depressed.

CEWLD

Query: If it is more blessed to give than to receive, why does the receiving humble us who have been givers?

MARCH 28

Luke 1:37–38

37 For with God nothing shall be impossible.
38 And Mary said, Behold the handmaid of the Lord; be it unto me according to thy word. And the angel departed from her.

Women—Christian and Islamic Attitude Toward

Islamic Theology, like the Christian, considered woman a main source of evil, which could be controlled only by her strict subordination. Children grew up in the discipline of the harem; they learned to love their mother and to fear and honor their father; nearly all of them developed self-restraint and courtesy. Good manners prevailed in all classes along with a certain ease and grace of motion probably derived from the women, who may have derived it from carrying burdens on their heads. The climate forbade haste, and sanctioned indolence.

Will & Ariel Durant,
Rousseau and Revolution: The Story of Civilization,
New York, Simon and Schuster, 1967, p. 416

Query: How do we learn to, as the song says, "guard each one's dignity and save each one's pride" ?

MARCH 29

Hebrews 12:3

3 For consider him that endured such contradictions of sinners against himself, lest ye be wearied and faint in your minds.

Inheritance (Cultural and Social)

The reading of history is, in some respects, very discouraging. This is particularly true of the history of human values, of the slow growth of human decency. What has been set forth by prophets, founders, social thinkers, and poets has repeatedly been distorted beyond recognition. Many of the "followers" of Jesus are actually worshipers of a cruel Oriental despot. They have made of Jesus a sadist, a merciless judge, a God who reflects their own selfishness and mean-ness. Even his own disciples got to arguing not about the impending Kingdom of Heaven but who would be the greatest, the Bigwig, the Bigshot. And they were vitally interested in who was going to rank the highest in Heaven. AND THESE WERE DISCIPLES–THE TWELVE–THE CLOSEST to Jesus.

Whether in religion or in politics or in concepts of The Good Society, always the tendency has been to distort, to warp, and at times to uphold the very opposite of what the Founder, or Prophet or Philosopher set forth.

At times one has to adopt stoicism or it would be impossible to continue living.

CEWLD

Query: Do we seek understanding, a legacy, a living, as reward for our virtue or do we wait for status in Heaven? If the latter, how does this affect our daily life on earth?

MARCH 30

Romans 12:10–13

10 Be kindly affectioned one to another with brotherly love; in honour preferring one another;
11 Not slothful in business; fervent in spirit; serving the Lord;
12 Rejoicing in hope; patient in tribulation; continuing instant in prayer;
13 Distributing to the necessity of saints; given to hospitality.

Human Decency

If you plan to translate into behavior as well as speech, the values of human decency (justice, honesty, sharing, love, sympathy, and the like) you must be prepared 'to be taken.'

CEWLD

Query: Is it better to be isolated than to give without taking, knowing that some/many may take advantage of you? (Note: CEWLD lived a solitary life but gave liberally to students and former students.)

MARCH 31

Hebrews 10:25

25 Not forsaking the assembling of ourselves together as the manner of some is; but exhorting one another: and so much the more as ye see the day approaching.

Human Relations

'Community,' said the sociologist Robert Nisbet, 'encompasses all form of relationships which are characterized by a high degree of personal intimacy, emotional depth, moral commitment, social cohesion, and continuity in time. Community is founded on man in his wholeness rather than in one or another of the roles, taken separately, that he may hold in a social order.'

Adam Smith,
In a review of H. Browne's *You Can Profit From a Monetary Crisis,*
Macmillan, 1974, [an obscene book on how to make money without having the slightest regard for your fellowmen.—CEWLD observation],
The New York Times Book Review, March 31, 1974, p. 7

Query: How possible is it for the stranger to succeed to the inmost circle of our intimate community?

⇒APRIL⇐

APRIL 1

Deuteronomy 7:9

9 Know therefore that the LORD thy God, he is God, the faithful God, which keepeth covenant and mercy with them that love him and keep his commandments to a thousand generations.

Light

'People talk a lot about Enlightenment and ask for more light…'

Lichtenberg [!] wrote, 'But my God, what good is all that light if people either have no eyes, or if those who do have eyes resolutely keep them shut?'

Immanuel Kant,
[Footnote Aphorism L 469, Aphorism, 1793–1799, 90]

Light, Visibility of

On a dark night, the human eye can see a burning candle 30 miles away.

Peter Farb,
Cited by Marvin Harris in a review of Farb's book,
Humankind (Boston, Houghton Mifflin),
The New York Times Book Review, March 18, 1978.

Query: Do we live fully by the Light we have?

APRIL 2

Job 11:15–18

15 For then shalt thou lift up thy face without spot; yea, thou shalt be stedfast, and shalt not fear;
16 Because thou shalt forget thy misery, and remember it as waters that pass away:
17 And thine age shall be clearer than the noonday; thou shalt shine forth, thou shalt be as the morning.
18 And thou shalt be secure, because there is hope; yea thou shalt dig about thee, and thou shalt take thy rest in safety.

Security

Throughout the historical period, the highest value for most human beings has been material security—survival in the flesh. Often enough love, happiness, integrity, human decency, truth, beauty—often enough, material security has been more important than anything and everything else. This is probably an inevitable consequence of socialization.
CEWLD

Query: Does our security depend on others or is it from our own inner resources?

APRIL 3

Matthew 10:16

16 Behold, I send you forth as sheep in the midst of wolves, be ye therefore wise as serpents, and harmless as doves.

Harmlessness (*Ahimsa*)

The only way we can maintain Harmlessness is to have Justice, to protect the Integrity of our fellow man and our own.

CEWLD

Query: When we interfere deeply in the fate of another, can we be certain to do it without harm?

APRIL 4

Luke 6:21

21 Blessed are ye that hunger now: for ye shall be filled. Blessed are ye that weep now, for ye shall laugh.

Seeing

The satiated man and the hungry one do not see the same thing when they look upon a loaf of bread.

Jalaluddi Rumi,
Cited by Idries Shah,
The Sufis,
Baltimore, Anchor, 1971, p. 141

Query: From whence does our sufficiency come?

APRIL 5

Deuteronomy 24:19

19 When thou cuttest down thy harvest in thy field, and hast forgot a sheaf in thy field, thou shalt not go again to fetch it: it shall be for the stranger, for the fatherless, and for the widow.

By the Book

No one can study the ancient languages in which the Bible is written without encountering problems which cannot be solved and without raising questions for which there are no final answers

Carl E.W.L. Dahlstrom,
1917–1919: a Personal History, p. 23,
Portland, 1980

Query: How does one measure generosity of spirit?

APRIL 6

I Peter 5:2–3

2 Feed the flock of God which is among you, taking the oversight thereof, not by constraint, but willingly: not for filthy lucre, but of a ready mind. 3 Neither as being lords over God's heritage, but being ensamples to the flock.

Necessity

Necessity is a powerful agent of compromise.

CEWLD

Necessity—2

This still recent youthful consciousness of power has led man to believe in the possibility of an eternity of bliss in some utopian paradise. But a maturer reality principle reveals these dreams to be as futile as the hope of perpetual motion; and this is true essentially as we have seen, for like thermodynamic reasons. That is why, perhaps, the wisest of men have stated in one form or another the principle of freedom in terms of necessity: to be free is to make a virtue of necessity.

Roderick Seidenberg,
Post-historic Man, An Augury,
(U. of N. Carolina, 1950),
New York, Viking, 1974, p. 169

Query: Is it our necessity we see or is it merely unrecognized Guidance?

APRIL 7

Galatians 6:9

9 Be not weary in well doing for in due season we shall reap if we faint not.

Sacred—2

The man of the archaic societies tends to live as much as possible IN the sacred or in close proximity to consecrated objects. The tendency is perfectly understandable, because, for primitives as for all pre-modern societies, the SACRED is equivalent to a POWER, and in the last analysis, to REALITY. The sacred is saturated with BEING. Sacred power means reality and at the same time enduringness and efficacy.

Mircea Eliade,
The Sacred and the Profane,
New York, Harcourt, Brace & World, 1959, p. 12

Query: Is there a boundary between the sacred and the service areas of our lives and is accomplishment in each rewarded differently?

APRIL 8

Romans 14:7–8

7 For none of us liveth unto himself, and no man dieth unto himself.
8 For whether we live, we live unto the Lord; and whether we die, we die unto the Lord: whether we live therefore or die, we are the Lord's.

Sacred

Every sacred space implies a *hierophany*, an irruption of the sacred that results in detaching a territory from the surrounding cosmic milieu and making it qualitatively different.

Mircea Eliade
The Sacred and the Profane,
New York, Harcourt, Brace & World, 1959 p, 12

Query: Why is it most of our epiphanies come outside the walls of the "place of worship"? Brother Lawrence experienced his while doing the dishes.

APRIL 9

Ecclesiastes 7:11–13

11 Wisdom is good with an inheritance: and by it there is profit to them that see the sun.
12 For wisdom is a defense, and money is a defense; but the excellency of knowledge is, that wisdom giveth life to them that have it.
13 Consider the work of God, for who can make that straight, which he hath made crooked?

Love

And you, men and women who sit in judgment, do you understand now that love, no matter how personal or universal, is not a solution? And that outside of love there is no solution?

Elie Wiesel,
A Beggar in Jerusalem, (1970),
New York, Avon, 1976, p. 172
Query: If God writes outside the lines He Himself has drawn, can we see it? What then?

APRIL 10

John 12:24

24 Verily, verily, I say unto you, Except a corn of wheat fall into the
ground and die, it abideth alone: but if it die, it bringeth forth much fruit.

Solitude

Socialization pulls man out of his life of solitude, which is his real and
authentic life.

Ortega y Gasset,
Man and Crisis, p. 99,
Translated by Mildred Adamo,
Cited by Joseph Campbell, *The Masks of God*,
New York, Viking, 1970, p. 390

Query: St. Francis was torn between the life of solitary prayer and the life
of preaching and service and he never quite resolved it. Do we feel that
tension?

APRIL 11

Romans 8:24–25

24 For we are saved by hope: but hope that is seen is not hope: for what a
man seeth, why doth he yet hope for it?
25 But if we hope for what we see not, then do we with patience wait for
it.

Hope

One must eventually arrive in his thinking at a place in which he gives up
all hope, all expectations, and at the same time does not register either
disappointment or despair. This is what various writers have told us. It is
true that the older you get, the more control you have of your responses
to experience. Yet can a living person have no hope and be wholly lacking
in despair? Is such a one a human being? Sometimes I have a vague
feeling as to what these people mean, but I am not sure. In their minds
they picture some figure of such control that he is virtually a god. Yet if a
god has no compassion, for example can he show any?
    We live on and on, the poets notwithstanding, because positive

expectations are greater than negative—otherwise life makes little or no sense.

CEWLD

Query: What were the positive expectations, if any, in Mary Magdalene and that other Mary and the women who had followed Jesus from Galilee as they approached the sepulcher on the morning of the first Easter?

APRIL 12

Job 42:10

And the LORD turned the captivity of Job, when he prayed for his friends; also the LORD gave Job twice as much as he had before.

Sacred

Religious man's desire to live…in the sacred…is in fact equivalent to his desire to take up his abode in objective reality, not to let himself be paralyzed by the never ceasing relativity of purely subjective experience, to live in a real and effective world, and not in an illusion. This behavior is documented on every plane of religious man's existence, but it is particularly evident in his desire to move about only in a sanctified world that is in a sacred space. This is the realm for the elaboration of techniques of … orientation … which properly speaking, are techniques for the … construction … of sacred space.

Mircea Eliade,
The Sacred and the Profane,
New York, Harcourt, Brace & World, 1959, pp. 23–24

Query: Is one protected when living, moving, having their being, in the "sacred space"?

APRIL 13

Judges 21:25

25 In those days there was no king in Israel: every man did that which was right in his own eyes.

Social Discontinuity

In all these lands, however divergent the political situation, the problem
was essentially the old one—whether the ancient system of one land and
one church could be abandoned without social chaos.

Roland H. Bainton,
The Reformation of the 16th Century,
Boston, Beacon, 1971, p. 141

Query: If anarchists have a convention, who would be their leader?

APRIL 14

Hebrews 5:4

4 And no man taketh this honour unto himself, but he that is called of
God, as was Aaron.

Honor

If a person's work honors him (her), the honor of his (her) fellow human
beings is superfluous. If a person's work does not honor him (her), then
the honor of his (her) fellow human beings is without foundation.
    Because of the above conditioning of 'honor,' some people of
substantial work will accept only the honors accompanied by significant
financial rewards.

CEWLD

Query: What is it which builds that which lasts?

APRIL 15

Proverbs 17:17

17 A friend loveth at all times, and a brother is born for adversity.

Friend

...einen Schein zu greifen, einen guten treuen,
beiständigen Freund zu finden, ist nahend gleich
müglich auf Erden worden.

To grasp a light is just as possible as to find on earth a
good loyal friend who'll stand by you.

Johannes von Saaz,
Der Ackermann,
[Saaz died 1414]

Query: Can we be friends, true friends, across the boundaries of age, class
and gender?

APRIL 16

Matthew 15:27–28

27 And she said, Truth, Lord: yet the dogs eat of the crumbs which fall
from their masters' table.
28 Then Jesus answered and said unto her, O woman, great is thy faith;
be it unto thee even as thou wilt. And her daughter was made whole from
that very hour.

Mother

And he, [Epicurus] is the first man in the record of European history
whose mother was an important element in his life. Some of his letters to
her have been preserved, and show a touch of intimate affection which of
course must have existed between human beings from the remotest times
but of which we possess no earlier record, and fragments of his letters to
his friends strike the same note.

Gilbert Murray,
Five Stages of Greek Religion, 3rd Ed. (1951),
Garden City, New York,
Doubleday (Anchor), 1955, p. 98

Query: Between mother and daughter, how is it today?

APRIL 17

Galatians 5:13

13 For brethren, ye have been called unto liberty; only use not liberty for an occasion to the flesh, but by love, serve one another.

Morality

    I. Is Not:

        A. Positive response to law and order; it is not legalism.
        B. Self-interest; it is not based on one's own good.

    II. Is:

        A. Concern for well being of others
        B. In action, it is the effort to maintain (protect), restore, or (in slavery) establish the integrity of others (the inviolability of a person's humanity).

CEWLD

Query: What does it take to restore another's choices…and then get out of the way?

APRIL 18

Job 4:12–13

12 Now a thing was secretly brought to me, and mine ear received a little thereof.
13 In thoughts from the visions of the night, when deep sleep falleth on men.

Social Classes

In a nomad civilization there are simply families. They may be rich or poor, but the tribe is not divided into different social classes. Some tribes are 'nobler' than others, but all Bedouin regard themselves as 'noble' compared with the settled cultivators. Even slaves do not constitute a class apart: they form part of the family.

Roland de Vaux,
Ancient Israel,
New York, McGraw-Hill, 1965, Vol. I. p. 68

Query: Do we have a role in an extended family and are we comfortable with it?

APRIL 19

Psalm 27:1

1 The Lord is my light and my salvation; whom then shall I fear? The Lord is the light of my life; of whom, then, shall I be afraid?

To Act in This World

Society itself, as I think I read, forty or fifty years ago, is only an abstraction, only a word for men, women, children and babies.

CEWLD

The Dahlstrom Interviews, Peter Jessen, Tape Two,
Transcribed by Rosalie V. Grafe

Query: What drives action? A mentor's advice? The dictates of civil authorities? Peer pressure? Confidence in the Inner Voice?

APRIL 20

Deuteronomy 4:32

32 For ask now of the days that are past, which were before thee, since the day that God created man upon the earth, and ask from the one side of heaven unto the other, whether there hath been any such thing as this great thing is, or hath been heard like it?

Past, The

What a pleasure it is to talk learnedly of the past—the more remote, the more learnedly! We fit together the few pieces that are available and then we sketch in the rest! In our ignorance and the lack of data, we can construct any number of pictures of the way we think things were.

Well, unless some disastrous loss occurs, the people of the future will have more data than they want. When they try to put them together, they will have many items that don't seem to fit. Perhaps it is just as well that much of our writing is on paper that will soon perish.

CEWLD

Query: What do we bring forward into today from yesterday? From last week? From last year? From our education? From our childhood?

APRIL 21

Nahum 1:7

7 The LORD is a good and a strong hold in the day of trouble; and he knoweth them that trust in him.

Truth and truth

1. The true is a fragment; Truth is the whole.
2. The true can be measured, weighed, counted, subjected to all procedures & measures to the examination of fragments. Truth is not subject to any of these procedures.
3. The true is publicly verifiable. Truth is not verifiable.
4. The true belongs to analytical thinking; Truth belongs to holistic thinking.
5. The true is determined according to a given frame of reference; Truth is an empathic response to the whole.
6. One can fill libraries and museums with books and devices for ascertaining and expressing what is true. On the other hand, we have no objective ways of presenting Truth; we can feel it, empathize it, and pursue it in liturgy and the fine arts, but we cannot objectify it.

CEWLD

Query: When faced with Jesus, Pilate asked: "What is Truth?"

APRIL 22

Psalm 84:3

3 Yea, the sparrow hath found an house, and the swallow a nest for herself, where she may lay her young, even thine altars, O LORD of hosts, my King, and my God.

Past, The

Inasmuch as we can never return to the past, we should limit ourselves to historical studies to learn what we can about our predecessors. Their successes, their mistakes, their failures may teach us some important lessons provided that we always remember that occurrences of the past were forces and products in a given context of circumstances. That context is never repeated … precisely … as it existed; hence one cannot treat the present situations with the same techniques that (in our hindsight) we would have used in the past.

CEWLD

Query: Do we understand, recall, learn from, the events of the past hour, the past day, the past week, and so on? Or is it rather a choice as to what we build on for the present?

APRIL 23

Jeremiah 29:11–13 (NIV)

11 'For I know the plans I have for you,' declares the LORD, 'plans to prosper you and not to harm you, plans to give you hope and a future.
12 Then you will call upon me and come and pray to me, and I will listen to you.
13 You will seek me and find me when you seek me with all your heart.'

Courtesy

Questioning another's motive violates one of the most respected taboos of courtesy—and a very necessary one, inasmuch as courtesy has the function of minimizing the arousal of aggression.

Erich Fromm
The Anatomy of Human Destructiveness (1968, 1969),
Greenwich, Conn., Fawcett, 1975, p. 233

Query: What is our response when we are led or advised to do something beyond our ability to understand?

APRIL 24

II Timothy 1:7

7 For God hath not given us the spirit of fear; but of power, and of love, and of a sound mind.

Fear

There is no philosophy possible where fear of consequences is a stronger principle than love of truth.

John Stuart Mill,
Cited by T.R. Glover,
Conflict of Religion in the Early Roman Empire,
Boston, Beacon, 1960, p. 90

Query: Can one follow Light and flee Darkness simultaneously?

APRIL 25

Acts 16:12–13

12 And from thence to Philippi, which is the chief city of that part of Macedonia, and a colony: and we were in that city abiding certain days.
13 And on the Sabbath we went out of the city by a river side, where prayer was wont to be made; and we sat down, and spake unto the women which resorted thither.

Fear

The most significant feature of man's golden age, according to Sumerian thinkers, was freedom from fear, or as the poet puts it:

> Once upon a time there was no snake, there was no scorpion,
> There was no hyena, there was no lion,
> There was no wild dog, no wolf,
> There was no fear, no terror,
> Man had no rival.

Samuel Noah Kramer,
The Sumerians,
University of Chicago, 1963, p. 262

Query: Do we worship fearlessly with those outside the norms of our conditioning and walls of our temples? Do we serve fearlessly with them?

APRIL 26

Romans 9:25–26

25 As he saith also in Osee, I will call them my people, which were not my people: and her beloved, which was not beloved.
26 And it shall come to pass, that in the place where it was said unto them, Ye are not my people, there shall they be called the children of the living God.

Fear

There is no philosophy possible where fear of consequences is a stronger principle than love of truth.

John Stuart Mill,
Cited by T.R.Glover,
Conflict of Religion in Early Roman Europe,
Boston, Beacon, 1960, p. 90

Query: Can one carry one's true identity without fear into and past one betrayal, two, more? What about into success?

APRIL 27

Job 38:18–19

18 Hast thou perceived the breadth of the earth? Declare if thou knowest it all.
19 Where is the way where light dwelleth? And as for darkness, where is the place thereof?

Light

Sometimes the light comforts us just by dispelling the dark. Sometimes we are frightened by what we see.

Sometimes the light shows what we can and must do. Sometimes the light tells us that we are victims who cannot lift a finger to effect our salvation.

No wonder that men worshipped sun, moon and stars.

Et Lux ista in tenebris lucet, sed tenebrae eam non comprehenderunt [John 1: 5].

CEWLD

Query: The colors of dawn and of sunset, are they the same?

APRIL 28

Joshua 24:15

15 And if it seem evil unto you to serve the LORD, choose you this day whom ye will serve: whether the gods which your fathers served that were on the other side of the flood, or the gods of the Amorites, in whose land ye dwell, but as for me and my house, we will serve the LORD.

Change and Chance

The world in which we are set is a world of change and chance in which nothing is ever perfected, nothing permanent, nothing secure. But the world can be understood: through the change of this world we can come to know truths.... The world as we experience it may be held to exist for the sake of leading minds to words. What is 'permanent', 'changeless' and 'perfect' in itself?

Karl Britton,
Philosophy and the Meaning of Life,
Cambridge University Press, 1969, p. 52

Query: What change does the light of morning reveal?

APRIL 29

John 17:26

26 And I have declared unto them thy name, and will declare it: that the love wherewith thou hast loved me may be in them and I in them.

Suffering

'May God save you not from suffering but from indifference to suffering,' my friend Moshe had wished me. [Azriel speaking].

Elie Wiesel,
The Oath (1973),
New York, Avon, 1974, p. 97

Query: Love and Light, how is it we trust them?

APRIL 30

Isaiah 6:8

8 Also I heard the voice of the LORD, saying, Whom shall I send and who will go for me? Then said I, Here am I; send me.

Confidence

It is a brave thing for any man, knowing his weakness, to stand firm for his principles against a stupid and brutal world.

George N. Kates,
The Years That Were Fat, The Last of Old China (1952),

Cambridge, Mass., MIT, 1967, p. 231

Query: Who has courage to follow the advice of a native person in a new country?
In the contexts of local laws and customs or past the point of common sense?

MAY

MAY 1

Psalm 31:24

24 Be of good courage, and he shall strengthen your heart, all ye that
hope in the LORD.

Courage

Man's worth lies in one thing only, in this, that he live and die bravely,
without condescending to accept any recompense. And I also know
this third requirement, which is more difficult yet: the certainty that no
recompense exists must not make our blood run cold, but must fill us
with joy, pride, and manly [sic] courage."

Nikos Kazantzakis,
Report to Greco,
New York, Simon and Schuster, 1965, p. 482

Query: Can we forge a legacy that will not have our name on it?

MAY 2

Proverbs 31:10, 29

10 Who can find a virtuous woman? For her price is above rubies.
29 Many daughters have done virtuously, but thou excellest them all.

Virginity in the Ancient World

As everywhere in the ancient world, virginity simply means not belonging to any man personally; virginity is in essence sacred, not because it is a state of physical inviolateness, but because it is a state of psychic openness to God....

The hero's birth is expressly attributed to a virgin.

Erich Neumann,
The Origin and History of Consciousness,
Princeton, 1971, p. 133

Query: Do we use our eyes to see and ears to hear—both inwardly and outwardly—this day?

MAY 3

Job: 11:18–19 [From Zophar's Discourse to Job]

18 And thou shalt be secure, because there is hope; yea, thou shalt dig about thee, and thou shalt take thy rest in safety.
19 Also, thou shalt lie down, and none shall make thee afraid; yea, many shall make suit unto thee.

Solomon's Reign

And Judah and Israel dwelt in safety, from Dan even to Beersheba, every man under his vine and under his fig tree, all the days of Solomon.

I Kings 4:25

(Apropos the part of the quotation on vine and fig tree, see also II Kings 18:31; Micah 4: 4)

CEWLD

Query: Can one work without the assurance of safety? How can one refrain from working nevertheless?

MAY 4

Isaiah 43:4

4 Since thou wast precious in my sight, thou hast been honourable, and I have loved thee: therefore will I give men for thee, and people for thy life.

Virtue

What is so wonderful about teaching the Humanities is the encounter with Virtue.

CEWLD

Query: If virtue is it's own reward, is that enough?

MAY 5

Proverbs 8:32

32 Now therefore hearken unto me, O ye children: for blessed are they that keep my ways.

Virtue

'Virtue is the absence of temptation.'

I first heard this from the mouth of Dr. Augustus Kirchner, dermatologist, whom I met as a medical student at the University of Michigan. It was in one of our conversations in Paris (1926 or 1927) that he said this; I do not know his source (common saying?)

CEWLD

Query: Is another person ever a means to an end?

MAY 6

Proverbs 4:7

7 Wisdom is the principal thing: therefore get wisdom: and with all thy getting, get understanding.

Wisdom and Happiness

Most people prefer happiness to wisdom; in fact, very few follow the injunction of the author of Proverbs to seek wisdom. Yet since happiness is so rare and at best fleeting, the seeking of wisdom is of the greatest value. It ennobles one to forego happiness and yet to be content with existence.

CEWLD

Query: Do you know a wise person?

MAY 7

Matthew 6:1—4

1 Take heed that ye do not your alms before men, to be seen of them: otherwise ye have no reward of your Father, which is in heaven.
2 Therefore when thou doest thine alms, do not sound a trumpet before thee, as the hypocrites do in the synagogues and in the streets, that they may have glory of men. Verily I say unto you, They have their reward.
3 But when thou doest alms, let not thy left hand know what thy right hand doeth.
4 That thine alms may be in secret: and thy Father, which seeth in secret himself shall reward thee openly.

Virtue

We like to make examples of people whose actions we don't like; we carefully avoid setting examples of people whose actions we do like (or pretend to like).

CEWLD

Query: Can virtuous acts done in secret compose a secret legacy?

MAY 8

I Samuel 12:24

24 Only fear the LORD and serve him in truth with all your heart; for consider how great things he hath done for you.

Probability

One can be completely optimistic about the possibilities—the way things work out on paper verbally and mathematically—and at the same time be totally pessimistic about the probabilities. The critical link between possibility and probability is the human factor.

CEWLD

Query: Do we insist on high probability of success or can we go experimentally forward in simple obedience to the Inner Voice?

MAY 9

Psalm 90:12–17

12 So teach us to number our days, that we may apply our hearts unto wisdom.
13 Return, O LORD, how long? And let it repent thee concerning thy servants.
14 O satisfy us early with thy mercy; that we may rejoice and be glad all our days.
15 Make us glad according to the days wherein thou hast afflicted us, and the years wherein we have seen evil.
16 Let thy work appear unto thy servants, and thy glory unto their children.
17 And let the beauty of the LORD our God be upon us and establish thou the work of our hands upon us; yea the work of our hands, establish thou it.

Time

We are able to deal with time only by making it static—so many seconds, minutes, hours etc. We have learned to split the second, of course, but not to remove the stasis in our manipulation of time.

Whatever ... time is ... it is a ceaseless irreversible flow or movement or alteration—a kinetic something. It seems to have something to do with absolute motion, because as a whole it cannot be measured.

CEWLD

Query: What does multi-tasking do to our ability to hear the Inner Voice while there is yet time?

MAY 10

Ecclesiastes 9:11

11 I returned and saw under the sun, that the race is not to the swift, nor the battle to the strong, neither yet bread to the wise, nor yet riches to men of understanding, nor yet favour to men of skill; but time and chance happeneth to them all.

Time

In the Continuum of Occurrence as a whole, there can be no distinction between past and future. I don't know if Time means anything more to the Continuum of Occurrence than a cosmic growling of the stomach.

CEWLD

Query: What differentiates today from yesterday or tomorrow and how much does that matter?

MAY 11

Psalm 30:4–5

4 Sing unto the LORD, O ye saints of his, and give thanks at the remembrance of his holiness.
5 For his anger endureth but a moment' in his favour is life: weeping may endure for a night, but joy cometh in the morning.

Time

It is disconcerting to discover that the one-way flow of time cannot be explained by the familiar principles of physics, which after all, are supposed to give us the deepest understanding of how the world works. All of the equations of motion are reversible in time.

Barry Commoner,
The Poverty of Power,
New York, Knopf, 1976, p. 9

Query: Can we remember in the night as well as in the morning that it "came…to pass"?

MAY 12

John 15:12–16

12 This is my commandment, That ye love one another, as I have loved you.
13 Greater love hath no man than this, that a man lay down his life for his friends.
14 Ye are my friends if ye do whatsoever I command you.
15 Henceforth I call you not servant for the servant knoweth not what his lord doeth; but I have called you friend for all things that I have heard of my Father I have made know unto you.
16 Ye have not chosen me, but I have chosen you, and ordained you that ye should go and bring forth fruit and that your fruit should remain; that whatsoever ye shall ask of the Father in my name, he may give it to you.

Time—Desert

The camel's sure, undulating rhythm transports your body, your blood takes on the rhythm of this undulation, and together with your blood, so does your soul. Time frees itself from the geometric subdivisions into which it has been so humiliatingly jammed by the sober, lucid mind of the West. Here with the rocking of the 'desert ship', time is released from its mathematical, firm-set confines; it becomes a substance that is fluid and indivisible, a light, intoxicating vertigo which transforms thought into reverie and music.

Nikos Kazantzakis,
Report to Greco,
New York, Simon and Schuster, 1965, p. 261

Query: Of that which we claim to have done "for God", what remains or will remain?

MAY 13

Psalm 43:3–4

3 O send out thy light and thy truth: let them lead me; let them bring me unto thy holy hill, and to thy tabernacles.
4 Then will I go unto the altar of God, unto God my exceeding joy: yea, upon the harp will I praise thee, O God my God.

Time—Christian

Christianity radically changed the experience and the concept of liturgical time, and this is due to the fact that Christianity affirms the historicity of the person of Christ. The Christian liturgy unfolds in a historical time sanctified by the incarnation of the Son of God. The sacred time periodically [restored] in pre-Christian religion (especially in the Arabic religions) is a mythical time that is, a primordial time, not to be found in the historical past, an original time, in the sense that it came into existence all at once, that it was not preceded by another, because no time could exist before the appearance of the reality narrated in the myth.

Mircea Eliade,
The Sacred and the Profane,
Harcourt, Brace & World, 1959 p. 72

Query: How is it we know when "the time has come" or "these things have been fulfilled"?

MAY 14

Lamentations 3:24–28

24 The LORD is my portion, saith my soul: therefore will I hope in him.
25 The LORD is good unto them that wait for him, to the soul that seeketh him.
26 It is good that a man should both hope and quietly wait for the salvation of the LORD.

27 It is good for a man that he bear the yoke in his youth.
28 He sitteth alone and keepeth silence because he hath borne it upon him.

Time—Sacred

For religious man of the archaic cultures, the world is renewed annually;
in other words, with each new year it recovers its original sanctity, the
sanctity that it possessed when it came from the Creator's hands.

Mircea Eliade,
The Sacred and the Profane,
Harcourt, Brace and World, 1959 p. 75

Query: We wait in hope, but can we wait without expectation of a known
or potential outcome?

MAY 15

Isaiah 42:18–20

18 Hear ye deaf; and look, ye blind, that ye may see.
19 Who is blind, but my servant or deaf, as my messenger that I sent?
Who is blind as he that is perfect, and blind as the LORD's servant?
29 Seeing many things, but thou observest not; opening the ears, but thou
hearest not.

Time—Sacred

The cosmogony is the supreme divine manifestation, the paradigmatic act
of strength, super-abundance and creativity. Religious man thirsts for the
real. By every means at his disposal he seeks to reside at the very source
of primordial reality….

Mircea Eliade
The Sacred and the Profane,
Harcourt, Brace & World, 1959 p. 72

Query: Can we hear God's voice from the mouth of a disliked stranger?

MAY 16

Psalm 145:14-15

14 The LORD upholdeth all that fall, and raiseth up all those that be bowed down.
15 The eyes of all wait upon thee: and thou givest them their meat in due season.

Ritual

This ritual re-actualization [making real and present once more] in which the first epiphany of a reality occurred, is the basis for all sacred calendars; the festival is not merely the commemoration of a mythical (and hence religious) event; it re-actualizes the event.

Mircea Eliade
The Sacred and the Profane,
Harcourt, Brace & World, 1959 p. 81

Query: Is there such a thing as a shared mystical experience?

MAY 17

Proverbs 16:32–33

32 He that is slow to anger is better than the mighty; and he that ruleth his spirit than he that taketh a city.
33 The lot is cast into the lap: but the whole disposing thereof is of the LORD.

Tentativism

All facts are tentative, but none are quite as tentative as those divulged by archaeology, and the further one goes back the more tentative they become.

Chaim Bermant and Michael Weitzman,
Ebla: A Revelation in Archaeology (1979)
Reviewed in *New York, Times Books,* 1979, p. 15

Query: When are we certain that we are not sure?

MAY 18

Psalm 90:12–17

12 So teach us to number our days, that we may apply our hearts unto wisdom.
13 Return, O LORD, how long? And let it repent thee concerning thy servants.
14 O satisfy us early with thy mercy; that we may rejoice and be glad all our days.
15 Make us glad according to the days wherein thou hast afflicted us, and the years wherein we have seen evil.
16 Let thy work appear unto thy servants, and thy glory unto their children.
17 And let the beauty of the LORD our God be upon u and establish thou the work of our hands upon us; yea the work of our hands establish thou it.

Obiter Dicta

Scattered throughout these files are personal comments of all kinds, ideas that I was moved to put on paper briefly, and perhaps a variety of obiter dicta. Do not be dismayed if you find me contradicting myself. I never made any contract to accept unconditionally today what I said yesterday.

I doubt if my comments are dated; hence I shall never know—nor will you—how to distinguish between 'yesterday' and 'today.'

CEWLD

Query: Could we greet each sunrise the same? Should we?

MAY 19

II Chronicles 20:20

20 …Believe in the LORD your God, so shall ye be established; believe in his prophets, so shall ye prosper.

Prosopolepsy

Per *Webster's International* (2nd ed), 'prosopolepsy' means 'acceptance of persons, esp. prematurely, from personal appearance.'
Think of this one word which says so much. But we have lost the word, such as it is, in the depths of the obsolete. After all, we can remember the many words of the definition more easily than the single word (especially since we no longer generally have any acquaintance with Latin and Greek).

...In Peter's opinion, [Acts 10:34] God does not succumb to prosopolepsy, no quick judgments on mere appearance. Or Peter might have said, God sees right through a person and instantly recognizes what is genuine and what is stance; pose, window dressing, mere appearance.

CEWLD

Query: What does God see to love in us? Can we see what he loves in the ones we cannot understand?

MAY 20

James 4:13–14

13 Go to now, ye that say, Today or tomorrow we will go into such a city, and continue there a year, and buy and sell, and get gain:
14 Whereas ye know not what shall be on the morrow....

The Future—Methods of Dealing With It

It must be recognized that there are other methods of dealing with the future than by projecting the past. Eating hash is one, or opening the pages of the Bible at random, or paying attention to dreams. I reject the first two methods for reasons based largely on personal experience; reasons which observation shows are not universally accepted. I also usually reject the third method, but not always, as when I find the solution to a problem of apparatus design in a dream.

P.W. Bridgman,
The Way things Are,
New York, Viking, 1961, p. 117

Query: What was your first conscious thought on rising in the morning?

MAY 21

Titus 1:5–9

5 For this cause left I thee in Crete, that thou shouldest set in order the things that are wanting, and ordain elders in every city as I had appointed thee:
6 If any be blameless, the husband of one wife, having faithful children not accused of riot or unruly.
7 For a bishop [elder] must be blameless, as the steward of God: not self-willed, not soon angry, not given to wine, no striker, not given to filthy lucre:
8 But a lover of hospitality a lover of good men, sober, just, holy, temperate;
9 Holding fast the faithful word as he hath been taught, that he may be able by sound doctrine both to exhort and to convince the gainsayers.

Decade, The: 1945–1955

No wonder it has been a difficult decade [failure of Russians and Americans to come to an understanding]. Yet the least we can expect is another one just as difficult, since the alternative is a nice clean planet with no people on it.

Herbert Agar, *The Price of Power*, (1957),
University of Chicago, 1965, p. 53

Query Do we advise or do we take advice? Both at once? Possible?

MAY 22

Proverbs 1:33

33 But whoso hearkeneth unto me shall dwell safely, and shall be quiet from fear of evil.

Contradiction:

Nomadic societies produced human beings of very similar mold; civilized societies have produced radical extremes of human beings ranging from the most intelligent, refined, and creative classes to the dull, brutalized, and incompetent classes.

How do we explain the reverse of … [this]? Perhaps it is a matter of energy available to nomads and permanent settlers. The nomads expend so much of their energy in order to get food (to stay alive) that they do not have time to consider social matters. They need to operate from a fixed social basis.

Is this not also true of the lowest economic classes in our civilized world? Is it not possibly true that the more energy one puts into work just to stay alive, the less is available for anything like the enhancement of survival? In civilized communities, the oppression of the lowest classes creates extra time (hence energy) for the other classes. The latter therefore have time to think and act on activities not immediately concerned with food. So chieftains of tribes want to become kings. Kings want to expand their lands and increase their wealth. The fever (the "gold-rush" fever?) seizes many and the turmoil of civilized life results.

Moral: If we want peace and quiet and changelessness, imitate the archaic nomad (no longer possible!); if we want to continue the search for the farthest reaches of human capabilities, we must accept the ceaseless turmoil of civilized life.

CEWLD

Query: Is peace incompatible with progress?

MAY 23

Psalm 146:13–16

13 Thy kingdom is an everlasting kingdom, and thy dominion endureth throughout all generations.
14 The LORD upholdeth all that fall, and raiseth up all those that be bowed down.
15 The eyes of all wait upon thee; and thou givest them their meat in due season.
16 Thou openest thine hand, and satisfiest the desire of every living thing.

Loneliness

Loneliness does not come from having no people about one, but from being unable to communicate the things that seem important to oneself, or from holding certain views which others find inadmissible.

C.G.Jung
Memories, Dreams, Reflections,
New York, Vintage, 1963, p. 356

Query: What are we to the passersby, to the powerful, to any other, and what does this matter to God?

MAY 24

Ecclesiastes 3:15

15 That which hath been is now; and that which is to be hath already been; and God requireth that which is past.

Continuum of Occurrence

The Continuum of Occurrence, the experience thereof, and the report of the experience are three separate and distinct phenomena. Unwittingly most people merge the three as though they were one.

CEWLD

The Uncharted surrounds us on every side and we must needs have some relation towards it, a relation which will depend on the general discipline of a man's mind and the bias of his whole character. As far as knowledge and conscious reason will go, we should follow resolutely their austere guidance.

Gilbert Murray,
Five Stages of Greek Religion, 3rd ed (1951),
Garden City, N.Y.,
Doubleday (Anchor), 1955, p. 164

Query: How do we affirm that which continues?

MAY 25

Ecclesiastes 11:1–5

1 Cast thy bread upon the water for thou shalt find it after many days.
2 Give a portion to seven and also to eight; for thou knowest not what
evil shall be upon the earth.
3 If the clouds be full of rain, they empty themselves upon the earth: and
if the tree fall toward the south, or toward the north, in the place where
the tree falleth, there it shall be.
4 He that observeth the wind shall not sow; and he that readeth the
clouds shall not reap.
5 As thou knowest not what is the way of the spirit, nor how the bones
do grow in the womb of her that is with child: even so thou knowest not
the works of God who maketh all.

Time—(Negative Time)

Some people have wanted to move back in historical time by circling the
globe at a speed faster than that of the globe itself revolving on its axis.
Success in the venture would require negative time. This means that on
each circuit one would have to end the trip before he began it, arrive
before he took off! A nice trick indeed! Moreover, if a pilot traveled in the
machine, he would eventually be unborn and if something happened to
make the machine inoperable, he who had been unborn would be unborn
forever! No wonder people enjoy science fiction.

CEWLD

Query: Imagine you could go back in time; how far would you go and
what would you change and what would be the consequences in the lives
interlocked with yours?

MAY 26

I Samuel 6:9

9 ... if so, it was chance that happened to us.

Probability—2

Probability is a statement about the likelihood of encountering some particular event among all the possible events that can occur.

Barry Commoner
The Poverty of Power,
New York, Knopf, 1976, p. 21

Query: Can we know when we are merely anonymous players in the story of another?

MAY 27

Hebrews 13:18

18 Pray for us for we trust we have a good conscience, in all things willing to live honestly.

Honesty

Here we are Catholics who don't cheat; Protestants who don't cheat; Jews who don't cheat; Freethinkers who don't cheat. That is why we are so few Catholics; so few Protestants; so few Jews; so few Freethinkers. And in all, so few of us. And against us we have the Catholics who cheat; the Protestants who cheat; the Jews who cheat; the Freethinkers who cheat—and that makes a lot of people. Besides this, all the cheats have a sureness in recognizing and standing by one another; an infallible sureness; an invincible sureness; to support each other; an un-atonable sureness. An instinctive sureness, a sureness pertaining to the race, the only instinct which they possess, comparable alone to the deep sureness with which the mediocre know and support the mediocre.... If only we honest people were faithful to honesty as mediocrity is faithful to mediocrity.

Charles Peguy,
Basic Verities (tr. From the French),
New York, Pantheon, 1943, p. 46

Query: In negotiations do we fully know what we gain or lose in closing a transaction?

MAY 28

Hebrews 13:1–3

1 Let brotherly love continue.
2 Be not forgetful to entertain strangers for thereby some have
entertained angels unawares.
3 Remember them that are in bonds, as bound with them: and them
which suffer adversity, as being yourselves also in the body.

Interdependence

As every archaeologist and every card player knows, what is visible is
linked with what is buried or unseen. We often go wrong interpreting the
visible when totally ignorant of that which is buried, unavailable, unseen,
irretrievable, inaccessible. We are likely to be still more in error if we
concentrate all our attention and efforts on what is visible.

CEWLD

Query: Is there a mirror to the invisible?

MAY 29

Proverbs 22:1–2

1 A good name is rather to be chosen than great riches, and loving favour
rather than silver and gold.
2 The rich and poor meet together: the LORD is the maker of them all.

Controls—Social

It is possible that people need to believe that they are managed if they are
to be managed effectively.

John Kenneth Galbraith,
The New Industrial State, 2nd ed.,
Houghton Mifflin, 1971, p. 220

Query: Whom do you call for permission? For approval?

MAY 30

Psalm 48:14

14 For this God is our God for ever and ever: he will be our guide, even unto death.

The Dead

Respect for the dead signifies respect for the living---respect for the continuity of the human community and recognition of each man's place within it.

Eugene D. Genovese,
Roll Jordan Roll,
New York, Pantheon Books, 1974, p. 202

Query: How do the ceremonies honoring the dead open new doors, new alliances?

MAY 31

Ecclesiastes 4:9–10

9 Two are better than one: because they have a good reward for their labour.
10 For if they fall, the one will lift up his fellow: but woe to him that be alone when he falleth; for he hath not another to help him up.

Hebrew

Hebrew thinking, until the Babylonian exile, was historical, although not eschatological. It always interpreted history—seeking out of its origin and consequence—although its understanding of Providence was rooted in the finitude of life and the exigencies of its natural and political environment. The Hebrew view of history, which prepared for and shaped the eschatology, which would arise out of catastrophe, was oriented to immanent fulfillment within history.

A. A.Cohen,
Myth of Judeo-Christian Tradition,
New York, Schocken, 1971, pp. 6–7

Query Can one endure catastrophe with only God's companionship and if so, can one learn the right lessons therefrom?

⪫JUNE⪪

JUNE 1

Job 1:21

21 …Naked came I out of my mother's womb, and naked shall I return thither: the LORD gave, and the LORD hath taken away; blessed be the name of the LORD.

Loneliness

On this earth we are 4 billion [1979] men, women, children, and babies. And never before has there been such a high percentage of utterly lonely people.

CEWLD

Query: Who sits with us when we deal with authority?

JUNE 2

James 5:10–12

10 Take, my brethren, the prophets who have spoken on the name of the LORD, for an example of suffering affliction, and of patience.
11 Behold, we count them happy which endure. Ye have heard of the patience of Job, and have seen the end of the LORD; that the LORD is very pitiful, and of tender mercy.
12 But above all things, my brethren, swear not, neither by heaven, neither by the earth, neither by any other oath: but let your yea be yea; and your nay, nay; lest ye fall into condemnation.

Virtue

The great word—there is a big critical and historical literature upon it—which seems to point up this mad scramble of all the talents—is the Italian *virtu*. The word, like our modern virtue , comes from the Latin *vir*, man. But Renaissance virtue emphasizes 'man' in the way our manliness does, and adds a great deal more. Like the ideals of chivalry from which it in part descends, virtu is an upper class ideal, to which a gifted person of lesser birth may indeed rise.

Crane Brinton
Shaping of Modern Thought,
Englwood Cliffs, Prentice-Hall, 1963, p. 40

Query: Do we give public vocal assent to words of which we are not certain?

JUNE 3

I Chronicles 11:17–19

17 And David longed, and said, Oh that one would give me drink of the water of the well of Bethlehem, that is at the gate!
18 And the three brake through the host of the Philistines, and drew water out of the well of Bethlehem, that was by the gate, and took it and brought it to David: but David would not drink of it, but poured it out to the LORD.
19 And said, My God forbid it me, that I should do this thing: shall I drink the blood of these men that have put their lives in jeopardy? For with the jeopardy of their lives they brought it. Therefore he would not drink it. These things did these three mightiest.

Virtus

What are the virtues which the Romans particularly admired? Firstly there is *virtus* itself. The world is often used in the speeches, and generally with a suggestion of stern and manly qualities; the ideal is the strong-minded, self-controlled man who can despise all pleasures and spend his life in bodily and mental exertion. The word *virtus* is sometimes joined with *constantia* and *gravitas*, those qualities on which the Roman so prided himself; associated with these is *magnitudo animi*, that lofty spirit which never yields to fortune or circumstances. Loyalty, trustworthiness, integrity, frugality and self-control complete the picture of the virtuous Roman.

M.L.Clarke,
The Roman Mind,
Cambridge, Mass., Harvard, 1956, p. 16

Query: Have we seen or can we lead the virtuous life in this current age?

JUNE 4

Psalm 78:39

39 For he remembered that they were but flesh; a wind that passeth away, and cometh not again.

Immortality

The fact … that immortality cannot be 'proved' is not very important, for nothing of any importance can be 'proved' anyway. All life is a matter of faith, and the task of the honest man is to find a reasonable faith.

David Elton Trueblood,
From the Foreword to *Spirit in Man*,
by Rufus Matthew Jones (1863–1948),
Stanford University, 1941, pp. viii–ix.

Query: Could you have believed past the first nail?

JUNE 5

I Samuel 2:35

35 And I will raise me up a faithful priest, that shall do according to that which is in mine heart and in my mind: and I will build him a sure house: and he shall walk before mine anointed for ever.

Immortality

A great part of the charm of oriental religions, on the study of which we are about to enter, lay in the assurance which they seemed to give of an immortal life.

Samuel Dill,
Roman Society from Nero to Marcus Aurelius,
New York, Meridian, 1956, p. 484

Query: How much does "eternal reward" feature in our motivation for serving those we encounter on a daily basis?

JUNE 6

Chronicles 6:32–33

32 Moreover concerning the stranger, which is not of thy people Israel, but is come from a far country for thy great name's sake, and thy mighty hand, and thy stretched out arm: if they come and pray in this house; 33 Then hear thou from the heavens, even from thy dwelling place, and do according to all that the stranger calleth to thee for; that all people of the earth may know thy people Israel, and may know that this house which I have built is called by thy name.

Human Needs

True fundamental needs of human existence: (a) that of the regulation and ordering of human relationships founded on a set of established values, skills and capabilities, truths and experiences; and (b) that of improvement of human existence by the securing of greater mastery over the natural environment, by extending knowledge of the surrounding reality, by obtaining a greater security and protection against hostile forces, by the reduction of human effort and by making human cooperation rest on a more balanced foundation.

Now, the first tendency is known to manifest itself with greatest strength in all those cultures, which rely exclusively on oral transmission, and direct demonstration in handing down their cultural contents and experience. The second, on the other hand, is apt to come to the fore in the crucial periods of social upheaval and revolution, which are known to have opened up new eras in human history.

Kazimierz Dobrowalski,
"Peasant traditional Culture,"

Ethnografia Polska, Vol I, 1958,
Excerpt tr. By A. Waligorski,
In Teodor Shamn,
Peasants and Peasant Societies,
Baltimore, Penguin, 1975, pp. 278–279.

Query: Are we bound up in our property and possessions so that we can
be bought and sold according to their disposition?

JUNE 7

Exodus 14:13–14

13 And Moses said unto the people, Fear ye not, stand still, and see
the salvation of the LORD, which he will shew to you today: for the
Egyptians whom ye have seen today, ye shall see them again no more for
ever.
14 The LORD shall fight for you, and ye shall hold your peace.

Human Suffering

Before the Neolithic Age, human beings suffered mostly from natural
ills—lack of sustenance, diseases, storms, earthquakes, floods, volcanic
eruptions and the like. Life was very difficult in archaic societies, and
those who reached old age were uncommon. During the historical period,
human beings have sought to overcome or avoid the ills of nature. In so
doing, however they have manufactured ills of their own. In fact, news
items constantly inform us that our own industrial world contaminates
everything. Recently, [1977] it was announced that it is dangerous for the
children to be breast fed by some of the mothers, so unwholesome—so
contaminated—is their milk.

Sometimes it seems that it is unsafe to eat anything, drink anything,
breathe the air, use appliances, or do anything at all. To the natural ills and
the industrial ills we have added all the psychological ills.

Do people lie awake nights trying to devise new ills or think up
new ways to frighten the world? We seem to live in an atmosphere of
manufactured fear. That reminds me that many, many years ago when
Camels, Lucky Strikes, and Chesterfields were the leading cigarettes,
someone started a rumor that one of the companies would hire only
Roman Catholics. Then came another rumor that another company
employed lepers to make cigarettes. I do not recall a third rumor. Things

just became too absurd to believe.

CEWLD

Query Can we stand open-eyed in that terrible place and having done all, still stand?

JUNE 8

Mark 8:35–37

35 For whosoever will save his life shall lose it; but whosoever shall lose his life for my sake and the gospel's, the same shall save it.
36 For what shall it profit a man if he shall gain the whole world and lose his own soul?
37 Or what shall a man give in exchange for his soul?

Contributions to the World of Humankind

LOVE
HAPPINESS
ENLIGHTENMENT
BEAUTY
PHYSICAL WELL BEING

I do not suggest any order or rank. Whoever contributes to one or more of these values adds greatly to the significance of human existence.

CEWLD

Query: Will today hold a possibility for a significant change? Can we see it?

JUNE 9

Hebrews 9:15

15 And for this cause he is the mediator of the new testament, that the means of death, for the redemption of the transgressions that were under the first testament, they which are called might receive the promise of

eternal inheritance.

Architect—Egyptian

The Egyptian architect was not the freely creative individual that is our own conception of an architect. The profession of architect in ancient Egypt was not even a distinct vocation. The Egyptian architect was first and foremost a court functionary, and he was frequently engaged in other occupations than architecture. In designing a building he possessed no creative will of his own but interpreted the will of the king, who in turn was the interpreter of tradition. Tradition was the rock on which the state was founded; to depart from it was to court calamity. The architect, like Pharaoh, was therefore not only the slave of tradition, but its willing slave.

Jon E. Manchip White,
Ancient Egypt, Its Culture and History (1952),
New York, Dover, 1970, p. 83

Query: What place do the Psalms of Imprecation have in our lives as followers of the Abrahamic Traditions?

JUNE 10

Isaiah 17:7

7 And at that day shall a man look to the Maker, and his eyes shall have respect to the Holy One of Israel.

Dead

Respect for the dead signifies respect for the living—respect for the continuity of the human community and recognition of each man's place within it.

Eugene D. Genovese,
Roll Jordan Roll,
New York, Pantheon Books, 1974, p. 202

Query: How can we best honor the beloved who are dead?

JUNE 11

Esther 8:6

6 For how can I endure to see the evil that shall come unto my people? or how can I endure the destruction of my kindred?

Yourself (The Stoic)

From time to time you have no alternative but to fall back on yourself; your own powers, your own capacities, be they great or small. The older you become, the more that death removes family and friends, the more alone you will be. Then comes the testing time, whether you can endure being so very much alone, whether your pride will prevent your revealing your sense of isolation, whether you have anything to fall back upon, whether you 'can take it.'

The scene changes constantly and visibly, but other changes are not equally manifest. On this or that occasion you become aware of the fact that you no longer fit into the world. You are a piece from a game that was completed some time ago. You do not belong. Have you the strength to take it? Will you break out in wrath against younger people and make them unhappy enough to wish that you were long since dead? Or will you somehow manage to live on your own resources whatever they may be?

CEWLD

Query: Who stays with us until the end? Can our own company suffice? Or can we form a new family; join a new community which will take us through the final phase?

JUNE 12

Psalm 34:22

22 The LORD redeemeth the soul of his servant and none of them that trust in him shall be desolate.

Torah

And in the small yeshiva where I would have stayed, indefinitely poring over the same page of the same book, I would never have imagined one could justify one's existence except by strictly observing the 613 commandments of the Torah.

Elie Wiesel,
One Generation After,
Texas, Bard, 1972, p. 223

Query: Are there periods in our lives we must still work to "justify" our desert experiences?

JUNE 13

Romans 14:1–8

1 Him that is weak in the faith receive ye, but not to doubtful disputations.
2 For one believeth that he may eat all things another, who is weak, eateth herbs.
3 Let not him that eateth despise him that eateth not; and let not him which eateth not, judge him that eateth: for God hath received him.
4 Who art thou that judgest another man's servant? To his own master he standeth of falleth. Yea, he shall be holden up: for God is able to make him stand.
5 One man esteemeth one day above another: another esteemeth every day alike. Let every man be fully persuaded in his own mind.
6 He that regardeth the day regardeth it unto the LORD and he that regardeth not the day, to the LORD he doth not regard it. He that eateth, eateth to the LORD, for he giveth God thanks; and he that eateth not, to the LORD he eateth not, and giveth God thanks.
7 For none of us liveth to himself, and no man dieth to himself.
8 For whether we live, we live unto the LORD; and whether we die, we die unto the LORD: whether we live therefore, or die, we are the LORD's.

Salvation

The restoration of the ideal order, which forms the original aim of creation, is also the secret purpose of existence. Salvation means actually nothing but restitution, re-integration of the original whole, or *Tikkun*, to use the Hebrew term.

G.G. Scholem,
Major Trends in Jewish Mysticism, 3rd Revised Edition,

New York, Schocken, 1961, p. 26

Query: Can we maintain our own fragmentation while seeking wholeness for the community?

JUNE 14

Romans 8:22

22 Hast thou faith? Have it to thyself before God. Happy is he that condemneth not himself in that thing which he alloweth.

Salvation

Islam: Together with silence, humility, and the remembrance of God, poverty is of great help toward the attainment of salvation. Worldly possessions are dangerous. 'Two bad companions, the Dinar and the Dorham! They profit you only when they leave you!' It is not so much poverty that is desirable but freedom from greed, avoidance of the temptations incident to wealth. The rich man is tied to this world with stronger cords than the poor. To be given a share in this world is likely to entail a threat to one's share in the next. The Prophet is represented as saying: 'The rich will be admitted to Paradise five hundred years later than the poor. Nothing', it is stated, 'of all the works that follow us, is more effective in obtaining for us a place in the other world, than renunciation of this world (*zuhd*).'

G.E. von Grunebaum,
Medieval Islam, 2nd Edition, (1953),
University of Chicago, 1971, pp. 127–128

Query: How is the decision made to invest the "top dollar", the "first fruits" of our labors?

JUNE 15

Deuteronomy 34:1–8

1 And Moses went up from the plains of Moab unto the mountain of Nebo, to the top of Pisgah, that is over against Jericho. And the LORD

shewed him all the land of Gilead, unto Dan,

2 And all Naphtali, and the land of Ephraim, and Manasseh, and all the land of Judah, unto the utmost sea,

3 And the south, and the plain of the valley of Jericho, the city of palm trees, unto Zoar.

4 And the LORD said unto him, This is the land which I sware unto Abraham, unto Isaac, and unto Jacob, saying, I will give it unto thy seed: I have caused thee to see it with thine eyes, but thou shalt not go over thither.

5 So Moses the servant of the LORD died there in the land of Moab, according to the word of the LORD.

6 And he buried him in a valley in the land of Moab, over against Beth-peor: but no man knoweth of his sepulcher unto this day.

7 And Moses was an hundred and twenty years old when he died: his eye was not dim, nor his natural force abated.

8 And the children of Israel wept for Moses in the plains of Moab thirty day so the days of weeping and mourning for Moses were ended.

Moses

The name Moses itself is Egyptian. It is the normal word for 'child' and occurs among the names, for example, of the pharaoh's of Dynasty XVIII. Years ago Edward Meyer suggested that in Moses' case the first part of the name—Ra-moses, Thut-moses, Ah-moses, or the like—may have been dropped, to obscure his Egyptian origin. And in any case the idea that an Egyptian princess could have thought the word to be Hebrew shows that the story tellers do not always think their problems through.

Joseph Campbell,
The Masks of God: Occidental Mythology,
New York, Viking 1971, p. 128

Query: How do we know when we have really come in out of the desert? Can we let go of the journey?

JUNE 16

Isaiah 16:2–3

2 For it shall be, that, as a wandering bird cast out of the nest, so the daughters of Moab shall be at the fords of Arnon.

3 Take counsel, execute judgment; make thy shadow as the night in the midst of the noonday; hide the outcasts; bewray not him that wandereth.

Law

Law was not born of the idea of justice, but of religion ... In order that there should be a legal relation between two men, it was necessary that there should already exist a religious relation; that is to say, that they should worship at the same hearth and have the same sacrifices.

Numa Denis Fustel de Coulanges (1830–1889),
The Ancient City, (1864); tr. English 1873)
Garden City, N.Y., Anchor, n.d., p. 173

Query: How does the Law speak to us of Grace?

JUNE 17

Exodus 24:7

7 And he took the book of the covenant and read in the audience of the people: and they said, All that the LORD hath said will we do, and be obedient.

Disciple

The term "disciple" is indicative of a form of education in which the student aligns him/herself with one teacher. For the most part, such alignment means subservience. The teacher is the Master; the disciple is the learner who tends to accept, *in toto*, the judgments and conclusions of the former. Plato and Aristotle had their followers; Jesus and Mohammad had their followers; Newton, Einstein, and Nils Bohr had their followers. Yet the scientific followers are not of the same order as the philosophers and the religious. Owing to the fact that the Humanities tend always toward the Holistic, the teachings of the Master are usually considered unimpeachable and unalterable. In the Sciences, however, tending as they always do toward the Analytical, the Master is eminent only for a position taken along the way. It is almost a rule that he expects to be surpassed and will be surpassed.

The Master-Disciple relationship reflects the old division of classes and ultimately the Master-Slave situation. It involved total obedience, total subservience, unquestioning acceptance of ideas and commandments.

CEWLD

Query: When is unquestioning obedience appropriate? To us? To another?

JUNE 18

I Kings 3:9–13

9 Give therefore thy servant an understanding heart to judge thy people,
that I may discern between good and bad: for who is able to judge this thy
so great a people?
10 And the speech pleased the LORD, that Solomon had asked this thing.
11 And God said unto him, Because thou hast asked this thing, and
hast not asked for thyself long life; neither hast asked riches for thyself,
nor hast asked the life of thine enemies; but hast asked for thyself
understanding to discern judgment;
12 Behold, I have done according to thy word lo, I have given thee a wise
and an understanding heart; so that there was none like thee before thee,
neither after thee shall any arise like unto thee.
13 And I have also given thee that which thou hast not asked, both riches,
and honour: so that there shall not be any among the kings like unto thee
all thy days.

Uniqueness

Most of us go through life thinking merely of people with variable
features, but all essentially alike. The physical anthropologist, perhaps
alone, is the most conscious of human differences, strange mutations
in the normal run of things, inexplicable emergences, atavisms, all
that difficult entangled thread that produces successive generations.
The hidden alphabet of life draws some characteristics into reality and
suppresses others. As the French biologist Jean Rostand has aptly put it,
'No man has a true counterpart.'

Loren Eiseley,
All the Strange Hours,
New York, Charles Scribners, 1975, p. 125

Query: Are we, in our uniqueness, a mirror for our opposite?

JUNE 19

Psalm 94:17

17 Unless the LORD had been my help, my soul had almost dwelt in silence.

Uniquity

Presumably no leaf or blade of grass or person or object exactly resembles another, but being unable to comprehend a world of unutterable and endless difference, we, as Aristotle said, put things into classes, and keep our sanity by speaking of oak tree or maple tree, man or woman, Frenchman or Englishman—just as if one of these quite resembled another. Hence it cannot be said that in Homer or Hemingway the object described indeed exists or that it quite corresponds to anything that we know. It only carries through a kind of faith the color of reality, and since we know that we exist and do see and touch things, it evokes the particularity that these things have.

John H. Finley, Jr.,
Four Stages of Greek Thought, (1966),
Stanford University Press, 1968, pp. 9–10

Query: To be seen, to be heard, to be understood; are these possible to givers or receivers of these gifts?

JUNE 20

Proverbs 29:18

18 Where there is no vision, the people perish: but he that keepeth the law, happy is he.

Decision

By *decision*, we do not mean accepting the decisions of others because of fear, because there is no alternative. One does not, for example, decide to send the blood through arteries.

Decision on the part of a unique individual must be uniquely determined by his whole being. Men are not machines of separate parts; they are organisms. With decision determined by the whole, unique creature, we have a strange manifestation of the determined as free!

CEWLD

Query: Does believing ever make it so? What changes when it doesn't?

JUNE 21

Psalm 118:19–24

19 Open to me the gates of righteousness I will go into them, and I will praise the LORD:
20 This gate of the LORD, into which the righteous shall enter.
21 I will praise thee: for thou hast heard me, and art become my salvation.
22 The stone which the builders refused is become the headstone of the corner.
23 This is the LORD's doing: it is marvelous in our eyes.
24 This is the day which the LORD hath made: we will rejoice and be glad in it.

Justice

William Godwin (1756–1836)

The fundamental principle of Godwin's political thought is that justice and happiness are indissolubly linked. 'The practice of virtue is the true road to individual happiness...,' he writes.

James Toll,
The Anarchists,
New York, Grossest & Dunlap, 1971, p. 32

Query: What is our response to injustice to ourselves? To our most dearly loved one? Are they the same response?

JUNE 22

John 1:5

5 And the light shineth in darkness; and the darkness comprehended it not.

Wisdom and Happiness

Most people prefer happiness to wisdom; in fact, very few follow the injunction of the author of Proverbs to seek wisdom. Yet since happiness is so rare and at best fleeting, the seeking of wisdom is of the greatest value. It enobles one to forego happiness and yet to be content with existence.

CEWLD

Query: Is wisdom imparted or does it grow within?

JUNE 23

Isaiah 26:3–4

3 Thou wilt keep him in perfect peace whose mind is stayed on thee: because he trusteth in thee.
4 Trust ye in the LORD forever: for in the LORD JEHOVAH [YWHW] is everlasting strength:

Uniqueness and Uniquity

Each of us possesses a unique composition that changes from moment to moment. Each of us carries also a unique genetic complement that, what with recessives that are not expressed and dominant genes that for some unknown reason withhold their effects, remains to a large degree, hidden. All of us bear hereditary potentials that we know nothing about and will never find anything about. Furthermore, we store history, a continuous flow of experience. When the time comes to make a decision, to exercise what we call free will, to choose—when that time comes, the self that exercises free will is, I think, that unique private self, that unique product of the unique composition, genetics and history, all to a degree unknown. At that moment no one can predict the outcome, neither an outsider nor the person making the decision, because no one has the requisite information. So I should say that the essence of free will is not a failure of determinism but a failure of predictability.

George Wold,
"Determinism, Individuality, And the Problem of Free Will"
In J.R.Platt,
New Views of the Nature of Man, 1965, ed.,
University of Chicago Press, 1970, pp. 36–37

Query: Obedience or avoidance, follow or lead, create a new way, or reference precedents and comply with majority opinion; how much of this is up to the individual to choose and to prioritize in life-altering decisions which affect integrity?

JUNE 24

Romans 16:19

19 For your obedience is come abroad unto all men. I am glad therefore on your behalf: but yet I would have you wise unto that which is good and simple concerning evil.

Evil

As long as one believes that the evil man wears horns, one will not discover an evil man.

Erich Fromm,
Anatomy of Human Destructiveness, (1973),
Greenwich, Conn., Fawcett, 1975, p. 480

It seems to me that many of us must be dangerously naïve if we think that evil people are readily recognizable, that is, "wear horns." But they are recognizable.

CEWLD

Query: Can one be "innocent concerning evil" and yet recognize it while avoiding harm?

JUNE 25

Isaiah 66:10–14

10 Rejoice ye with Jerusalem, and be glad with her, all ye that love her:
rejoice for joy with her, all ye that mourn, mourn for her:
11 That ye may suck, and be satisfied with the breasts of her consolation
that ye may milk out, and be delighted with the abundance of her glory.
12 For thus saith the LORD, Behold, I will extend peace to her like a river,
and the glory of the Gentiles like a flowing stream: then shall ye suck, ye
shall be borne upon her sides, and be dandled upon her knees.
13 As one whom his mother comforteth, so will I comfort you; and ye
shall be comforted in Jerusalem.
14 And when ye see this, your heart shall rejoice, and your bones shall
flourish like an herb: and the hand of the LORD shall be known toward
his servants, and his indignation toward his enemies.

Mother Image

In relation to the ego, the mother image has both a productive and
a destructive aspect, but over and above that, it preserves a certain
immutability and eternality. Although it is two-faced and can assume many
shapes, for the ego and consciousness it always remains the world of the
origin, the world of the unconscious. In general, therefore, the mother
represents the instinctual side of life, which compared with the changing
positions of the ego and consciousness proves to be constant and
relatively unalterable, whether it be good of bad, helpful and productive,
or hurtful and terrible. Whereas man's ego and his consciousness have
changed to an extraordinary degree during the last six thousand years,
the unconscious, the Mother, is a psychic structure that would seem
to be fixed eternally and almost unalterably. Even when the mother
image takes on the character of the spiritual mother, Sophia, it retains
its unchangingness, for it is an embodiment of the everlasting and all-
embracing, the healing, sustaining, loving and saving principle. It is eternal
in a sense quite different from that in which the father image is eternal.
The transformations and developments in the creative background are
in unconscious symbolism, always correlated with masculine mobility
and dynamism as expressed in the Logos-Son. In comparison with him,
the mover and the moved, Sophia is maternally quiescent. This is clearly
revealed in modern psychology, where the significance of the personal
mother is eclipsed by the mother archetype to a far greater degree than is
the case with the personal father. The mother image is less conditioned by
the temporal and cultural pattern.

Erich Neumann,
The Origins and History of Consciousness,
Princeton, 1971, p. 171

Query: Why are Comfort and Consolation causes for female imagery of God?

JUNE 26

Psalm 92:4–5

4 For thou, LORD, hast made me glad through thy work: I will triumph in the works of thy hands.
5 O LORD, how great are thy works! And thy thoughts are very deep.

Gratitude

Is there a prayer for pray-ers? If not, it should be invented. Leah told him [Moshe, her husband] one day: 'I am grateful to you not only for what you do and what you are, but also for what I am. I am grateful to you for that very gratitude. And Moshe answered her: 'I like what you just said, but you must never say it again.' And Leah understood. At the end of the word there is silence, at the end of silence there is the gaze.

Elie Wiesel,
The Oath, (1973),
New York, Avon, 1974, p. 176

Query: If God alone understands, is that sufficient?

JUNE 27

Psalm 68:4–6

4 Sing unto God, sing praises to his name: extol him that rideth upon the heavens by his name JAH, and rejoice before him.
5 A father of the fatherless, and a judge of the widows, is God in his holy habitation.
6 God setteth the solitary in families he bringeth out those which are bound with chains but the rebellious dwell in a dry land.

Gratitude—2

To expect gratitude in return for a good deed or a benefaction of any kind is to transform the operation into a commercial venture.

CEWLD

Query: *Quid pro quo* or "seventy times seven,"? Reparations, forgiveness— or grace?

JUNE 28

Isaiah 40:21–25

21 Have ye not known? Have ye not heard? Hath it not been told you from the beginning? Have ye not understood from the foundations of the earth?
22 It is he that sitteth upon the circle of the earth, and the inhabitants thereof are as grasshoppers; that stretcheth out the heavens as a curtain, and spreadeth them out as a tent to dwell in:
23 That bringeth the princes to nothing: he maketh the judges of the earth as vanity.
24 Yea, they shall not be planted; yea, they shall not be sown: yea, their stock shall not take root in the earth: and he shall also blow upon them, and they shall wither, and the whirlwind shall take them away as stubble.
25 To whom then will ye liken me, or shall I be equal, saith the Holy One.

Soul—Reality of

The reality of all cultures, our own included, consists in realizing these images which lie dormant in the psyche. All art, religion, science, and technology, everything that has ever been done, spoken, or thought, has its origin in this creative center the creative process of psychic *palingenesis* [or self-birth]. The self-generating power of the soul is man's true and final secret, by virtue of which he is made in the likeness of God the creator and distinguished from all other living things. These images, ideas, values, and potentialities of the treasure hidden in the unconscious are brought to birth and realized by the hero in his various guises—savior and man of action, seer and sage, founder and artist, inventor and discoverer, scientist and leader.
   It seems to be a well-established fact that the problem of creation lies

at the heart of the mythological canon which once prevailed throughout the Near East: everywhere the drama of the dying and resurgent god, enacted on New Year's Day by the king as the god's successor, the current creation story.

Erich Neumann,
History of Consciousness,
Princeton, 1971, pp. 210–211

Query: Through what actions does the soul speak and who interprets the message?

JUNE 29

Psalm 143:5–6

5 I remember the days of old: I meditate on all thy works; I muse on the work of thy hands.
6 I stretch forth my hands unto thee: my soul thirsteth after thee, as a thirsty land. Selah.

Soul—Reality of

The reality of the soul is one of the basic and most immediate experiences of mankind; it permeates primitive man's whole view of life, naturally without his being aware that it is an inner experience. The animating principle of manna, the effect of magic, the magical efficacy of spirits, and the reality of collective ideas, dreams, and ordeals are all governed by the laws of this interior reality which modern depth psychology is trying to bring to the surface. We must not forget that the discovery of the objective, external world is a secondary phenomenon, the result of human consciousness endeavoring, with infinite labor and the help of the instruments and abstractions of modern science, to grasp the object as such, independently of the primary reality of man, which is the reality of the psyche. But early man relates himself above all to this primary reality of psychic dominants, archetypes, primordial images, instincts, and patterns of behavior. This reality is the object of his science, and his efforts to deal with it in his cults and rituals were just as successful in controlling and manipulating the inner forces of the unconscious, as are modern man's efforts to control and manipulate the forces of the physical world.

Erich Neumann,
The Origins and History of Consciousness,
Princeton, 1971, pp. 209–210

Query: What of our soul continues in our kin, in our friends, and in the legacy of our work?

JUNE 30

Luke 6:35

35 But love your enemies, and do good, and lend, hoping for nothing again, and your reward shall be great, and ye shall be the children of the Highest: for he is kind unto the unthankful and to the evil.

Matthew 6:44–46

44 But I say unto you, Love your enemies, bless them that curse you, do good to them that hate you, and pray for them which despitefully use you, and persecute you;
45 That ye may be the children of your Father which is in heaven; for he maketh his sun to rise on the evil and on the good and sendeth rain on the just and the unjust.
46 For if ye love them which love you, what reward have ye? Do not even the publicans the same?

Gratitude—True

First you have to learn not to want gratitude. Then you have to learn not to want gratitude. Finally you have to learn that whatever you do, you do it because it is something that ought to be done.

CEWLD

Query: Prayers, alms-giving and loving action, do we list them in our accomplishments? For a community or church report? In a sermon?

⌒JULY⌒

JULY 1

Isaiah 40:21–25

21 Have ye not known? Have ye not heard? Hath it not been told you from the beginning? Have ye not understood from the foundations of the earth?
22 It is he that sitteth upon the circle of the earth, and the inhabitants thereof are as grasshoppers; that stretcheth out the heavens as a curtain, and spreadeth them out as a tent to dwell in:
23 That bringeth the princes to nothing: he maketh the judges of the earth as vanity.
24 Yea, they shall not be planted; yea, they shall not be sown: yea, their stock shall not take root in the earth: and he shall also blow upon them, and they shall wither, and the whirlwind shall take them away as stubble.
25 To whom then will ye liken me, or shall I be equal," saith the Holy One.

Forgiveness

It is not too difficult to say, 'I forgive you.' What is difficult is for one's behavior to demonstrate conclusively: 'You are forgiven.'

CEWLD

Query: Must at-one-ment precede communication with the Holy? Are there examples where it did not? Must we "understand" God to achieve atonement?

JULY 2

Psalm 27:4

4 One thing have I desired of the LORD, that will I seek after; that I may dwell in the house of the LORD all the days of my life, to behold the beauty of the LORD, and to enquire in his temple.

Starvation

Starvation disintegrates character even more than fear of violent death. The effects of starvation can never be wholly understood by someone who has not starved. Elie Wiesel saw a son kill his own father for a small piece of bread; he saw another father steal food from his own son who was too weak to move from his bunk to line up for his rations.

Peter Phillips,
The Tragedy of Nazi Germany,
New York, Pegasus, 1970, p. 195

Query In the blending of endings into beginnings, how can we see to move with confidence?

JULY 3

Judges 24:14–16

14 Now, therefore, fear the LORD, and serve him in sincerity and in truth: and put away the gods which your fathers served on the other side of the flood, and in Egypt; and serve ye the LORD.
15 And if it seem evil unto you to serve the LORD, choose you this day whom ye will serve; whether the gods which your fathers served that were on the other side of the flood, or the gods of the Amorites, in whose land ye dwell: but for me and my house, we will serve the LORD.
16 And the people answered and said, God forbid that we should forsake the LORD to serve other gods.

Simplicity

...the doctrine that our remote forefathers being simple folk had simple law dies hard. Too often we allow ourselves to suppose that, could we but get back to the beginning, we should find that all was intelligible and should then be able to watch the process whereby simple ideas were smothered under subtleties and technicalities. But it is not so. Simplicity is the outcome of technical subtlety; it is the goal not the starting point. As we go backwards the familiar outlines become blurred; the ideas become fluid and instead of the simple we find the indefinite.

Frederic William Maitland, Historian,
Ed. By Robert L. Schuyler,
University of California, Berkeley,1960 pp. 95–96.
Quoted from Maitland's *Domesday Book and Beyond* (1897)

Query: What are our first three priorities and how can we serve them today?

JULY 4

Proverbs 10:3

3 The LORD will not suffer the soul of the righteous to famish:

Simplicity—2

Assuming human nature to be a simple thing, the Enlightenment also, as a rule, assumed political and social problems to be simple, and therefore easy of solution.

Arthur O. Lovejoy,
The Great Chain of Being, (1936)
New York, Harper, 1960, p. 9

Query: How is righteousness recognized in the life and example of a human being?

JULY 5

Proverbs 8:1–12

1 Doth not wisdom cry? And understanding put forth her voice?
2 She standeth in the top of high places, by the way in the places of the paths.
3 She crieth at the gates at the entry of the city, at the coming in at the doors.
4 Unto you, O men, I call: and my voice is to the sons of men.
5 O ye simple, understand wisdom: and ye fools, be ye of an

understanding heart.

6 Hear; for I will speak of excellent things; and the opening of my lips shall be right things.

7 For my mouth shall speak truth and wickedness is an abomination to my life.

8 And the words of my mouth are in righteousness; there is nothing forward or perverse in them.

9 They are all plain to him that understand, and right to them that find knowledge.

10 Receive my instruction, and not silver; and knowledge rather than choice gold.

11 For wisdom is better than rubies; and all the things that may be desired are not to be compared to it.

12 I wisdom dwell with prudence, and find out knowledge of witty inventions.

Wisdom and Happiness

Most people prefer happiness to wisdom; in fact, very few follow the injunction of the author of Proverbs, to seek wisdom. Yet since happiness is so rare and at best fleeting, the seeking of wisdom is of the greatest value. It enobles one to forego happiness and yet to be content with existence.

CEWLD

Query: Of Wisdom, Wit and Prudence, which is the most practical of employment in the pursuit of Wholeness…or can they be separately pursued?

JULY 6

Judges 21:24–25

24 And the children of Israel departed thence at that time, every man to his tribe and to his family, and they went out from thence every man to his inheritance.

25 In those days there was no king in Israel: every man did that which was right in his own eyes.

Tribalism

Solomon [Ruth's great-great-great grandson] began to consolidate his power by means of a rigid reorganization of the kingdom. Twelve districts were established to be supervised by royal officials, two of whom were Solomon's sons-in-law. These districts were designated to supply monthly the prerequisites of the royal court in monies, food, material, and labor battalions. The king showed an astuteness in this endeavor, if one may call 'astute' those actions to weaken any opposition. The newly created districts cut across the traditional tribal borders and loyalties. This was obviously done to render ineffectual all tribal hostility to the growing bureaucracy in Jerusalem.

Marvin Berry, "The Age of Solomon,"
in *The Ancient World*, ed. By Raymond F. Lock, Los Angeles,
Los Angeles, Mankiad Publishing Co., 1970,
(The above essay published by Mankiad in 1967), p. 22

Comment

(1) Solomon was a tenth century B.C.E. figure
(2) 'Monies' collected by Solomon did not include what we mean by 'money,' for coinage first appeared during the 7th century B.C.E.
(3) Berry does not seem to understand that Solomon was engaged in compulsory assimilation, inasmuch as the Hebrews asked for a king, the egalitarians of the nomadic tribes no longer existed. The only way that Solomon could make a nation was by breaking up the tribes, making all Hebrews first and tribal members second, preferably not at all.

CEWLD

Query: Spiritual mediators and temporal leaders, are they ordained by God?

JULY 7

Mark 8:34–38

34 And when he had called the people unto him with his disciples also, he said unto them, Whosoever will come after me, let him deny himself, and take up his cross and follow me.
35 For whosoever will save his life shall lose it: but whosoever shall lose

his life for my sake and the gospel's, the same shall save it.
36 For what shall it profit a man if he shall gain the whole world and lose
his own soul?
37 Or what shall a man give in exchange for his soul?
38 Whosoever therefore shall be ashamed of me and of my words in this
adulterous and sinful generation; of him also shall the Son of man be
ashamed, when he cometh in the glory of his Father with the holy angels.

Tribe and City

The tribe, like the family ... was established as an independent body, since
it had a special worship from which the stranger was excluded. Once
formed, no new family could be admitted to it. No more could two tribes
be fused into one; their religion was opposed to this. But just as several
[households] were united in a tribe, several tribes might associate together,
on condition that the religion of each should be respected. The day on
which this alliance took place the city existed.

Numa Denis Fustel de Coulanges (1830–1889),
The Ancient City, (1864; 1873 tr. Engl.),
Garden City, New York, Anchor, n.d., pp. 126–127

Query: Our intimate circle, how far does it extend and how impermeable
are its borders?

JULY 8

Jeremiah 21:8

8 And unto this people thou shalt say, Thus saith the LORD; Behold, I set
before you the way of life, and the way of death.

Refugees

We had quite a colony of Belgian refugees [WWI] living in the parish
of Tor. Everyone had been bursting with loving-kindness and sympathy
when they arrived.
  People had stocked houses with furniture for them to live in, had done
everything they could to make them comfortable. There had been the
usual reaction later, when the refugees had not seemed to be sufficiently
grateful for what had been done for them and complained of this and

that. The fact that the poor things were bewildered and in a strange country was not sufficiently appreciated.

Agatha Christie,
Poirot's First Case,
Dodd, Mead, 1958,
[In an excerpt from her *Autobiography*, Dodd, Mead, Nov. 1977]
The New York Times Magazine, Sept.18, 1977, p. 42

Query: Why does the charity of strangers make us uneasy?

JULY 9

Isaiah 51:14

14 The captive exile hasteneth that he may be loosed, and that he should not die in the pit, nor that his bread may fail.

Existence

The late philosopher Morris R. Cohen of CCNY was asked by a student in the metaphysics course, ' Professor Cohen, how do I know that I exist?' The keen old prof replied, 'And WHO is asking?'

Saul Bellow,
Humbolt's Gift,
New York, Avon, 1976, p. 157

Query: If, as Descartes states, "I think, therefore I am." then what would the statement "I believe, therefore I ———" indicate once the blank was filled in to your satisfaction?

JULY 10

Proverbs 11:17–19

17 Bow down thine ear, and hear the words of the wise, and apply thine heart unto my knowledge.
18 For it is a pleasant thing if thou keep them within thee;
they shall withal be fitted to thy lips.

19 That thy trust may be in the LORD, I have made known to thee this day; even to thee.

Social Discontinuity

It is the first step in sociological wisdom, to recognize that the major advances in civilization are processes which all but wreck societies in which they occur....

Alfred North Whitehead,
Symbolism,
New York, Capricorn, 1955, p. 88

Query: In times of social change, what are our duties to those we encounter who do not have the eyes to see and yet have the power to hurt?

JULY 11

Job 11:15–18

15 For then shalt thou lift up thy face without spot; yea, thou shalt be stedfast, and shalt not fear:
16 Because thou shalt forget thy misery, and remember it as waters that pass away:
17 And thine age shall be clearer than the noonday; thou shalt shine forth, thou shalt be as the morning.
18 And thou shalt be secure, because there is hope; yea, thou shalt dig about thee, and thou shalt take thy rest in safety.

Social Discontinuity—2

An Ijo man was asked by a Christian missionary to abandon his old gods. He replied, 'Does your God really want us to climb to the top of a tall palm tree and then take off our hands and let ourselves fall?' Wherever established tenets have an absolute and exclusive validity, Horton comments 'any challenge to them is a threat of chaos, of the cosmic abyss, and therefore evokes intense anxiety.'

Basil Davidson,
The African Genius,

Boston, Little, Brown & Co., 1969, p. 178

Query: Is it ever appropriate to stand alone, and
if so, for how long?

JULY 12

Joshua 1:9

9 Have not I commanded thee? Be strong and of a good courage; be not
afraid, neither be thou dismayed: for the LORD thy God is with thee
whithersoever thou goest.

Social Discontinuity

'My generation,' wrote Dewey's colleague, James H. Tufts 'has seen the
passing of systems of thought which had reigned since Augustus. The
conception of the world as a kingdom ruled by God, subject to his
laws and their penalties, which had been undisturbed by the Protestant
Reformation, has dissolved.... The sanctions of our inherited morality
have gone. Principles and standards which had stood for nearly two
thousand years are questioned.'

Henry Steele Commager,
The American Mind,
Yale, 1950, p. 406
[N.B. Alfred North Whitehead made some such comment in one of his
essays.]

Query: How do we know when to seek new answers?

JULY 13

Haggai 1:3–11

3 Then came the word of the LORD by Haggai the prophet, saying,
4 Is it time for you, O ye, to dwell in your ceiled houses, and this house lie
waste?
5 Now therefore thus saith the LORD of hosts; Consider your ways.
6 Ye have sown much, and bring in little; ye eat, but ye have not enough;

ye drink, but ye are not filled with drink; ye clothe you, but there is none warm; and he that earneth wages earneth wages to put it into a bag with holes.

7 Thus saith the LORD of hosts; Consider your ways.

8 Go up to the mountain, and bring wood, and build the house; and I will take pleasure in it, and I will be glorified, saith the LORD.

9 Ye looked for much, and, lo, it came to little; and when ye brought it home, I did blow upon it. Why, saith the LORD of hosts. Because of mine house that is waste, and ye run every man unto his own house.

10 Therefore the heaven over you is stayed from dew, and the earth is stayed from her fruit.

11 And I called for a drought upon the land, and upon the mountains, and upon the corn, and upon the new wine, and upon the oil, and upon that which the ground bringeth forth, and upon men, and upon cattle, and upon all the labour of the hands.

Human Individualism

... rugged individualism has always possessed a big commanding voice whereas humane individualism has been silenced by torture, imprisonment, exile, mutilation and death.

CEWLD

Query: Am I my brother's keeper?

JULY 14

Psalm 69:20

20 Reproach hath broken my heart; and I am full of heaviness and I looked for some to take pity, but there was none; and for comforters, but I found none.

Blessings and Ills

A religious song admonishes us to 'count your blessings, name them one by one.' The tendency, however, is to dwell on our "ills," to magnify them when they are small and to be overwhelmed by them when they are large and laming.

CEWLD

Query: Can we bless the fire that refines us?

JULY 15

Deuteronomy 34:1–8

1 And Moses went up from the plains of Moab unto the mountain of Nebo, to the top of Pisgah, that is over against Jericho. And the LORD shewed him all the land of Gilead, unto Dan,
2 And all Naphtali, and the land of Ephraim, and Manasseh, and all the land of Judah, unto the utmost sea,
3 And the south, and the plain of the valley of Jericho, the city of palm trees, unto Zoar.
4 And the LORD said unto him, This is the land which I sware unto Abraham, unto Isaac, and unto Jacob, saying, I will give it unto thy seed: I have caused thee to see it with thine eyes, but thou shalt not go over thither.
5 So Moses the servant of the LORD died there in the land of Moab, according to the word of the LORD.
6 And he buried him in a valley in the land of Moab, over against Beth-peor: but no man knoweth of his sepulcher unto this day.
7 And Moses was an hundred and twenty years old when he died: his eye was not dim, nor his natural force abated.
8 And the children of Israel wept for Moses in the plains of Moab thirty day so the days of weeping and mourning for Moses were ended.

Moses

We have already seen that Abraham and his family came from Ur in Sumer to Hebron in Canaan, probably about 1850 B.C.E. and there are good reasons for placing Joseph's migration to Egypt during the Hyksos period (1700–1580 B.C.E.). For at least four centuries those who now called themselves 'Israelites' lived, multiplied and prospered in the Nile delta, until they were driven out by a Pharaoh 'whose heart the Lord had hardened'—more probably Rameses II (1290–1224 B.C.E.) than his successor, Mernephtah.

A man of supreme intelligence and powerful personality, the first great religious reformer in the history of humanity, Moses united the Israelites around the cult of a unique and universal God, led their long march across the Sinai peninsula and died when they reached the threshold of the 'Promised Land.'

Georges Roux,
Ancient Iraq, (1964)
Baltimore, Penguin, 1972, p. 242

Query: How do we know when we have really come in out of the desert? Can we let go of the journey?

JULY 16

Isaiah 42:16

16 And I will bring the blind by a way that they knew not; I will lead them in paths that they have not known: I will make darkness light before them, and crooked things straight. These things will I do unto them, and not forsake them.

Paths

Each child of man goes stumbling along paths it chose but did not make.

CEWLD

Query: Is it harder to walk by faith if we have "eyes to see"?

JULY 17

Ecclesiastes 12:11–12

11 The words of the wise are as goads, and as nails fastened by the masters of assemblies, which are given from one shepherd.
12 And further, by these, my son, be admonished: of making many books there is no end: and much study is a weariness of the flesh.

Communications [1967]

The size and magnitude of modern [1966] communications is staggering. The Defense Communications System, a world-wide strategic network of the American armed forces, transmits well over a quarter of a million messages a day, or more than 10,000 messages every hour. Its 10,000,000-plus channel miles—enough to circle the globe 400 times—are distributed among 85 subordinate nets that provide 25,000 channels and pass through 200 relay stations and more than 1,500 tributary stations. Its plant is worth $2.5 billion and it costs nearly three quarters of a million dollars a year to run. Operating it are more than 30,000 soldiers, sailors, and airmen.

David Kahn,
The Code-Breakers,
New York, Macmillan, 1967, p. 672
[Arpanet, the first Internet, Ed.]

Query: How do we learn what God is doing elsewhere?

JULY 18

Psalm 32:6–8

6 For this shall every one that is godly pray unto thee in a time when thou mayest be found: surely in the floods of great waters they shall not come nigh unto him.
7 Thou art my hiding place; thou shalt preserve me from trouble; thou shalt compass me about with songs of deliverance. Selah.
8 I will instruct thee and teach thee in the way which thou shalt go: whose mouth must be held in with a bit and bridle, lest they come near unto thee.

Community

Community is a corner of society where the individual can feel some confidence of acceptance on fairly honest terms and can maintain continuing association with others whose familiarity is comforting. Community provides a mooring for the spirit. For community is a restraint that liberates. It relieves us of the necessity to continually prove our worth or to seek reassurance of that worth. It diminishes the destructive social process of judging and being judged which cripples our capacity to think and act freely with honesty. Members of a community may not be friends, but they are not strangers. Even though interests and careers have diverged, many people retain a special affection for the companions of youth. They are the relics of that classroom community which is the last many have known.

Richard N. Goodwin,
The American Condition, (1974),
New York, Bantam, 1975, p. 75

Query: When do I cease to be just "I" and become part of "us"?

JULY 19

Ecclesiastes 7:20–25

20 For there is not a just man upon earth, that doeth good and sinneth not.
21 Also take no heed unto all words that are spoken; lest thou hear thy servant curse thee:
22 For oftentimes also thine own heart knoweth that thou thyself likewise hast cursed others.
23 All this have I proved by wisdom: I said I will be wise; but it was far from me.
24 That which is far off, and exceedingly deep, who can find it out?
25 I applied mine heart to know, and to search, and to seek out wisdom, and the reason of things, and to know the wickedness of folly, even of foolishness and madness.

Personal Makeup

Few men and women have any difficulty identifying the intelligent creature within them, the significant human being, the good neighbor, and the like. What takes all the wit and courage that anyone possesses is to identify the fool in oneself. It is a subject over which one is not inclined to linger. Even a fleeting glance is humiliating, discouraging, and frightening.

CEWLD

Query: Is our identity resident solely in ourselves or is it composed of how we are seen by others...or both?

JULY 20

Genesis 49:22–25

22 Joseph is a fruitful bough, even a fruitful bough by a well; whose branches run over the wall:
23 The archers have sorely grieved him, and shot at him, and hated him:
24 But his bow abode in strength, and the arms of his hands were made strong by the hands of the mighty God of Jacob; (from thence is the shepherd, the stone of Israel;)
25 Even by the God of thy father, who shall help thee; and by the Almighty who shall bless thee with blessings of heaven above, blessings of the deep that lieth under, blessings of the breasts, and of the womb:

Will

A strong will not only manifested a strong conscience (*liang-hsin*); it was also a measure of human immortality. Martyrs lost their mortal lives, but the spirit of their will was preserved to influence later generations. Moreover, the ideals defended by that will, should not be sacrificed to any form of authority. When Confucius wrote that 'the will even of a common man cannot be taken from him,' he was not denying one's responsibility to society. Rather, like some modern ethical philosophers, he meant that '… man belongs to a society and so must devote himself to the profit of his society.' If there is a time when his own interest and society's interests conflict, then he must sacrifice his own interest to society's. However, even though it is permissible to sacrifice one's own interest, it is not permissible to sacrifice one's own ideals. To be unwilling to give up one's own ideals is what was meant by not being able to take away even the will of an ordinary man.'

Quote from Yang Ch'ang-chi (1870–1920),
Professor of Ethics, Psychology, Education,
First Normal School [China].
Found in:
Frederic Wakeman, Jr.
History and the Will, (1973)
University of California, Berkeley, 1975, p. 163

Query: How much believing does it take to make it so?

JULY 21

Acts 2:17–18

17 And it shall come to pass in the last days, saith God, I will pour out my Spirit upon all flesh: and your sons and your daughters shall prophesy, and your young men shall see visions, and your old men shall dream dreams
18 And on my servants and on my handmaidens I will pour out in those days of my Spirit; and they shall prophesy:

Dream and Legend

But man cannot live indefinitely without a dream and without a legend. Therefore, if someone appears who brings them both—it is enough. He will impose himself and reign.

Elie Wiesel,
Souls on Fire,
New York, Vintage, 1973, p. 23

Query: How much of what we dream is under our control or initiated from our lives?

JULY 22

Psalm 25:15–18

15 Mine eyes are ever toward the LORD; for he shall pluck my feet out of the net.
16 Turn thee unto me, and have mercy upon me; for I am desolate and afflicted.
17 The troubles of my heart are enlarged. O bring thou me out of my distresses.
18 Look upon mine affliction and my pain; and forgive all my sins.

Wisdom

Wisdom is peculiar to the individual; it dies or disappears as the individual dies or disappears.
   Knowledge can be packaged, duplicated, preserved, passed on from generation to generation.
   One can be wise with little or no formal schooling; so too one can have extensive formal schooling and have access to great bodies of knowledge

without ever becoming wise....

CEWLD

Query: Can we both pursue wisdom and flee from folly?

JULY 23

Isaiah 54:4–8

4 Fear not; for thou shalt not be ashamed: neither be thou confounded;
for thou shalt not be put to shame: for thou shalt forget the shame of thy
youth, and shalt not remember the reproach of thy widowhood any more.
5 For thy Maker is thine husband; the LORD of hosts is his name; and
thy Redeemer the Holy One of Israel; The God of the whole earth shall
he be called.
6 For the LORD hath called thee as a woman forsaken and grieved in
spirit, and as a wife of youth when thou wast refused, saith thy God.
7 For a small moment have I forsaken thee; but with great mercies will I
gather thee.
8 In a little wrath I hid my face from thee for a moment; but with
everlasting kindness will I have mercy on thee, saith the LORD thy
Redeemer.

Beliefs

How often, when we study carefully our fondest beliefs, they turn out to
be products of social, psychological, and intellectual conditioning. We
are all caught in the webs of human cultures and human make-up. It is
not a little ironic that the more we try to escape, the more enwebbed we
may find ourselves. It is difficult for us to realize that we have to make
do with what we are and what we have. It is, of course, some kind of
accomplishment to learn that one is conditioned. Then it may be easier
to deal rationally and humanely with one's fellowmen, fellowwomen,
fellowchildren, fellowgrandparents, fellowparents, fellowsiblings,
fellowoffspring, and fellowfellows!

CEWLD

Query: From whom are we disconnected?

JULY 24

Lamentations 5:1–5

1 Remember, O LORD, what is come upon us consider, and behold our reproach.
2 Our inheritance is turned to strangers, our houses to aliens.
3 We are orphans and fatherless, our mothers are as widows.
4 We have drunken our water for money; our wood is sold unto us.
5 Our necks are under persecution: we labour and have no rest.

Shame

In an experience of shame, trust is seriously jeopardized or destroyed. Emphasis may fall on one side or the other: on the questioning of one's adequacy or on the questioning of the values in the world of reality which so contradict what one has been led to expect. Or both may be doubted. In any case, suddenly exposed discrepancy threatens trust. Part of the difficulty in admitting shame to oneself arises from reluctance to recognize that one has built on false assumptions about what the world one lives in is and about the ways others will respond to oneself.

Helen Merrell Lynd,
"On Shame and the Search for Identity," New York, 1950,
Cited by Eugene D. Genovese,
Roll Jordan Roll,
New York, Pantheon, 1972, p. 121

Query: Is there still learning from the unhealed wounds of shame?

JULY 25

Psalm 25:21

21 Let integrity and uprightness preserve me; for I wait on thee.

'Upperclasser' and 'Lowerclasser' (Criminals)

1. The 'upperclasser,' spending some months or years in prisons or jails, emerges, writes books, lectures, makes money. Often he

receives much sympathy, even admiration.

2. The 'lowerclasser,' spending some months or years in prisons or jails, emerges, is poor, cannot
find a job, and soon he is back in custody. Often enough he is viewed with contempt or loathing.

CEWLD

Query: Are the walls that restrain us of our own making or are they imposed?

JULY 26

Psalm 73:12–17

12 Behold, these are the ungodly, who prosper in the world; they increase in riches.
13 Verily I have cleansed my heart in vain, and washed my hands in innocency.
14 For all the day long have I been plagued, and chastened every morning.
15 If I say, I will speak thus; behold, I should offend against the generation of thy children.
16 When I thought to know this, it was too painful for me;
17 Until I went into the sanctuary of God; then understood I their end.

Dreams

For each age is a dream that is dying
or one that is coming to birth.

Arthur William Edgar O'Shaughnessy

Dreams—2

There is a dream dreaming US.

A Bushman hunter to Laurens Van der Post,
The Heart of the Hunter,
New York, William Morrow, 1961, p. 149

Dreams—3

> I cannot accept
> The real as real:
> Then how do I accept
> A dream as a dream?

Priest Saigyo (1118–1190)
The Penguin Book of Japanese Verse,
Baltimore, Penguin, 1964, p. 100

Query: Does following dreams build or create reality?

JULY 27

I Kings 4:32–34

32 And he spake three thousand proverbs and his songs were a thousand
and five.
33 And he spake of trees, from the cedar tree that is in Lebanon even
unto the hyssop that springeth out of the wall: he spake also of beasts,
and of fowl, and of creeping things, and of fishes.
34 And there came of all people to hear the wisdom of Solomon, from all
kings of the earth, which had heard of his wisdom.

Writers

The best writers remember that we learn with the ear as with the eye, and
even when writing solely for the printed page, they read their material to
themselves to root out ungainly constructions. They have it read back
to themselves as well. The ear will catch the false note, the effect not
achieved, the garbled syntax, the unintended repetition, the unconscious
and unwanted alliteration, where the eye does not.

Robin W. Winks,
The Historian as Detective, (1968, 1969)
Edited by Robin W. Winks,
New York, Harper & Row, 1970, p. 301

Writers —2

1. Those that write to earn a living
2. Those that write to entertain (often combined with No. 1)
3. Those that write so as to change others or society or the world
4. Those that write in an effort to gain a place in history
5. Those that write in order to impress 'the world' with their greatness
6. Those that write so as to create art
7. Those that write to communicate something to others
8. Those that write because they like to read that which has been composed by a superb, highly intelligent writer
9. Those that write because they are ordered to do so
10. Those that write to provide examples of calligraphy
11. Those that write so that they can clarify their own thinking

Obviously these classes can also exist in various combinations with one another. Taken altogether, they can be combined in half a billion ways. Thus there is reason enough for anyone to be a writer!

CEWLD

Query: Ruth's legacy was a written Bible book about her (The Book of Ruth) and her legacy was her descendants, the kings David and Solomon. Do we know what our legacy will be? Is it important that we know?

JULY 28

Isaiah 29:18–21

18 And in that day shall the deaf hear the words of the book, and the eyes of the blind shall see out of obscurity, and out of darkness.
19 The meek also shall increase their joy in the LORD, and the poor among men shall rejoice in the Holy One of Israel.
20 For the terrible one is brought to naught, and the scorner is consumed, and all that watch for iniquity are cut off:
21 That make a man an offender for a word, and lay a snare for him that reproveth in the gate and turn aside the just for a thing of naught.

Mysticism—'Empty'

In terms of immediate perception, when we look for things there is nothing but mind, and when we look for mind there is nothing but things. For a moment we are paralyzed, because it seems that we have no basis for action, no ground underfoot from which to take a jump. But this is the way it always was, and in the next moment we find ourselves as free to act, speak, and think as ever, yet in a strange and miraculous new world from which 'self' and 'other', 'mind' and 'things' have vanished. In the words of Te-shan: 'Only when you have no thing in your mind, and no mind in things are you vacant and spiritual, empty and marvelous.'

Alan W. Watts,
The Way of Zen,
New York, Vintage, 1957, p. 137

Query: Can one better see the light unto one's path with closed eyes?

JULY 29

Isaiah 29:9–12

9 Stay yourselves, and wonder; cry ye out, and cry: they are drunken, but not with wine; they stagger, but not with strong drink.
10 For the LORD hath poured out upon you the spirit of deep sleep, and hath closed your eyes; the prophets and your rulers, the seers hath he covered.
11 And the vision of all is become unto you as the words of a book that is sealed, which men deliver to one that is learned, saying, Read this, I pray thee: and he saith, I cannot; for it is sealed:
12 And the book is delivered to him that is not learned, saying, read this, I pray thee: and he saith I am not learned.

Mystery—Its Advent

When does mystery enter human consciousness? What is its association with religion, magic, purification, propitiation, outwitting the gods, and the like?
What is the difference between the sense of mystery of a member of an archaic society and that of a modern man …? Is it the difference between a belief in magic and a profound pursuit of science?

CEWLD

Query: When we are overwhelmed, can we still sense and follow the mystery?

JULY 30

Acts 11:21–26

21 And the hand of the Lord was with them: and a great number believed, and turned unto the Lord.
22 Then tidings of these things came unto the ears of the church which was in Jerusalem: and they sent forth Barnabas, that he should go as far as Antioch.
23 Who, when he came, and had seen the grace of God, was glad and exhorted them all, that with purpose of heart they would cleave unto the Lord.
24 For he was a good man, and full of the Holy Ghost and of faith: and much people were added unto the Lord.
25 Then departed Barnabas to Tarsus, for to seek Saul:
26 And when he had found him, he brought him unto Antioch. And it came to pass, that a whole year they assembled themselves with the church, and taught much people. And the disciples were called Christians first in Antioch.

Folly

Whether you set out to do good or to do evil, the probabilities are that you commit folly. It is therefore of the highest importance that we keep defining good and evil throughout our lives. Indeed, we have to be 'moral' in our doing good if we are to avoid doing evil. We must constantly keep in mind the concepts of 'harmlessness' and 'justice.' And this requires us to have intelligence, experience, understanding, knowledge.

CEWLD

Query: Can we serve the needs of others without connecting that service to our own enhancement or career goals? What happens when the serving conflicts with our career goals or self-enhancement?

JULY 31

Psalm 20:4–7

4 Grant thee according to thine own heart, and fulfill all thy counsel.
5 We will rejoice in thy salvation, and in the name of our God we will set up our banner the LORD saveth his anointed: he will hear him from his holy heaven with the saving strength of his right hand.
7 Some trust in chariots, and some in horse but we will remember the name of the LORD our God.

Mystic, The

The mystic, as it were, forestalls the processes of history by anticipating, in his own life, the enjoyment of the last age.

Charles Bennett
Cited by G.G. Scholem,
Major Trends in Jewish Mysticism, 3rd Edition,
New York, Schocken, 1961, p.20

Query: Can we go back by going forward?

≈AUGUST≈

AUGUST 1

Deuteronomy 3:24

24 O Lord God, thou hast begun to shew thy servant thy greatness, and thy mighty hand: for what God is there in heaven or in earth, that can do according to thy works, and according to thy might?

Righteousness

1. The righteousness of an individual determined by the group: Is this an index to a group-centered society?
2. The righteousness of an individual as produced by his own consciousness: Is this an index to an individual-oriented society?

What happened to the hunger and thirst for righteousness? The question assumes that the hunger and thirst have existed, something we are no longer sure of. But if it did exist, it is gone. The religious are smugly self-satisfied, self-righteous. The others, including many members of religious sects, hunger and thirst for affluence, comfort, convenience, ease, entertainment, including sports, and sex frolics, hetero- or homo-, whatever the mood of the moment. In the past, man has always been an animal, as he still is, but he at least aspired to be different from the other animals, to be indeed human. Now [1978] there seems almost a studied effort in all departments of life to demonstrate Mephistopheles' comment—man uses his intelligence to demonstrate that he is more bestial than any beast. (Goethe's Faust)

CEWLD

Query: How do we repair the consequences of unrighteous behavior?

AUGUST 2

Genesis 2:7

7 And the LORD God formed man of the dust of the ground, and breathed into his nostrils the breath of life; and man became a living soul.

Soul and Body

The distinction between soul and body is something foreign to the Hebrew mentality, and death, therefore, is not regarded as the separation of the two elements. A live man is a living 'soul', *nephesh,* and a dead man is a dead 'soul' a dead *nephesh* (Nb 6:16; Lev. 21:11; cf Nb. 19:13). Death is not annihilation. So long as the body exists and the bones at least remain, the soul exists, like a shade, in a condition of extreme weakness, in the subterranean abode of Sheol (Jb 26: 5–6; Is 14: 9–10 Ez 32: 17–32).

Roland de Vaux,
Ancient Israel,
New York, McGraw-Hill, 1965, p .56

Query: How do body and soul connect?

AUGUST 3

I Corinthians 15:45

45 And so it is written, The first man Adam was made a living soul; the last Adam was made a quickening spirit.

Soul—The Soul as BREATH

Hebrew: *Ruach*
Greek: *Psyche*
Latin: *Anima*
Sumerian: *lil*

Between heaven and earth they recognized a substance which they called *lil*, a word whose approximate meaning is wind, air, breath, spirit....

   Egyptian: Soul, the *ka*; the *ba* ; the *khu* ; the *sahu*

   Websters International (2nd): *sahu*...The incorruptible or spiritual body, in contrast to the *khet*.

   The *khet* is the mortal, objective body. I [CEWLD] cannot determine if the breath of *khet* evolves into the spirit of *sahu*.

Yo-Yo Ma, cellist: 'My parents taught me to believe in the soul that something extra which in Chinese is called *ling huen*, the beautiful part of human nature....'

Leslie Rubinstein,
"Oriental Musicians Come of Age."
The New York Times Magazine,
November 23, 1980, p. 82

Query: What are the true windows to the soul? Eyes? Actions? Loves? Children? Life stories?

AUGUST 4

Jonah 1:8

8 Then said they unto him, Tell us, we pray thee, for whose cause this evil is upon us; What is thine occupation? And whence comest thou? What is

thy country? And of what people art thou?

Identity

1. The organic man is what his genes make him.
2. The social man is what his human surround makes him.
3. The rational man is what his thinking makes him.
4. The spiritual man is what his sense of awe makes him.
5. The whole man is a product of all the external forces and internal forces that fashion him. The whole man is beyond analysis whether by himself or by others.

The alien is the human being who has no identity. He is Cain, cut off from all others because of his murderous behavior. The chief figure in *The Wanderer* laments the loss of all human associations.

   Identity, as said earlier in brief form, is a conviction, a certainty, that one belongs, that he has anchorage, *est enim sicut arbor plantata ad rivas aquarium* (Psalm 1:3) 'And he shall be like a tree planted by the rivers of water, that bringeth forth his fruit in his season; his leaf also shall not wither; and whatsoever he doeth shall prosper.' (KJV), he and 'the other' are forever bound together. He/she belongs (1) to a family, (2) to a larger group of human beings, (3) to God, (4) to him/herself, (5) to 'Destiny,' etc. Insofar as a person identifies himself as 'belonging' he cannot suffer alienation. Consider 'belonging to nothingness [or] to the whole.'

CEWLD

Query: How does one put down roots and how long does it take?

AUGUST 5

Psalm 14:6

6 Ye have shamed the counsel of the poor, because the LORD is his refuge.

Vocabularies

We speak and write and think in the vocabularies of individual experience. Words and thought structures of words are often identical to those employed by the other men and women of our society. The meanings, however, are often different. Thus we listen to someone or read what he has written; we are familiar with all the words and the ways in which they are put together. Yet we are puzzled and often ask, 'What does he mean?,' 'What is he saying?'

CEWLD

Query: How important are labels for our occupations, pre-occupations and loves?

AUGUST 6

Isaiah 11:10

10 And in that day there shall be a root of Jesse, which shall stand for an ensign of the people; to it shall the Gentiles seek; and his rest shall be glorious.

Wisdom

The wise know that the individual is not and cannot be free and therefore, in expressing the will of God…they become free. He who would gain his life must lose it….

W. I. Thompson
At the Edge of History,
New York, Harper (1971) p. 120

Query: Can the wise understand the past, weigh the present and prepare for the future … or how much should they or we labor to do so?

AUGUST 7

Psalm 119:109–112

109 My soul is continually in my hand: yet do I not forget thy law.
110 The wicked have laid a snare for me: yet I erred not from thy precepts.
111 Thy testimonies have I taken as an heritage for ever: for they are the rejoicing of my heart.
112 I have inclined mine heart to perform thy statutes always, even unto

the end.

Truth and the Individual

In terms of the total field, an individual cannot be a container of the truth; his action can only embody certain aspects of the truth. He can act out his role as superb tragedy or comedy, but he can never be the truth. The truth is what emerges on the field of the sphere as one man engages his opposite in conflict. This is precisely Yeats's very Greek tragic vision, and is what he saw shortly before he died when he wrote to a friend that man could never know the truth, he could only embody it so the truth could be seen in him by someone, God or Daimon, looking at history from the 'outside.'

William Irwin Thompson,
At the Edge of History,
New York, Harper (1971), 1972, p. 116

Query: When our truth is derided by another, how do we respond?

AUGUST 8

Luke 24:10–11

10 It was Mary Magdalene and Joanna, and Mary the mother of James, and other women that were with them, which told these things unto the apostles.
11 And their words seemed to them as idle tales and they believed them not.

Truth

Because an individual cannot contain the truth means that only the ignorant claim to be free. The wise understand exactly what a world weighs down upon them. And so we have a paradox: the ignorant scream that they are free of the tragedy and in claiming to be liberated individuals can never truly be so. The wise know that the individual is not and cannot be free and therefore, in expressing the will of God ... they become free. He who would gain his life must lose it....

W.I. Thompson

At the Edge of History
New York, Harper, 1971, p. 120

Query: Do the wise know that they are so?

AUGUST 9

I Timothy 1:5

5 Now the end of the commandment is charity out of a pure heart, and of a good conscience, and of faith unfeigned:

Wholeness

A great deal of Sufi poetry, in addition to its formal contents, refers to degrees of wholeness or ability to concentrate the mind and as a result find a way to the place where truth is not fragmented.

Sheikh el-Muskaikh
Cited by Idries Shah,
The Sufis,
Garden City, N.Y., Anchor, 1971, p. 341

Query: Can we permanently join our whole self to another in friendship or in love?

AUGUST 10

Psalm 18:28

28 For thou wilt light my candle; the LORD my God will enlighten my darkness.

Now

The technique of historical study itself demands that we shall look upon each generation as, so to speak, an end in itself, a world of people existing in their own right. All of which led the great German historian Ranke, a hundred years ago, to the important thesis that every generation is equidistant from eternity.

So the purpose of life is not in the far future, nor, as we so often imagine, around the next corner, but the whole of it is here and now, as fully as ever it will be on this planet. It is always a 'Now' that is in direct relation to eternity—not a far future; always, immediate experience of life that matters in the last resort—not historical existence based on abridged textbooks or imagined visions of some posterity that is going to be the heir of all the ages.

Herbert Butterfield,
Christianity and History,
New York, Scribners, 1959, pp. 65–66

Query: How is it that we bring out truth from each other by the present practice of ongoing friendship and then trust in our deepest connections?

AUGUST 11

John 15:7–17

7 If ye abide in me, and my words abide in you, ye shall ask what ye will, and it shall be done unto you.
8 Herein is my Father glorified, that ye bear much fruit; so shall ye be my disciples.
9 As the Father hath loved me, so have I loved you: continue ye in my love.
10 If ye keep my commandments, ye shall abide in my love: even as I have kept my Father's commandments, and abide in his love.
11 These things have I spoken unto you, that my joy might remain in you, and that your joy might be full.
12 This is my commandment, That ye love one another, as I have loved you.
13 Greater love hath no man than this, that a man lay down his life for his friends.
14 Ye are my friends, if ye do whatsoever I command you.
15 Henceforth I call you not servants, for the servant knoweth not what his lord doeth, but I have called you friends; for all things that I have heard of my Father I have made known unto you.
16 Ye have not chosen me, but I have chosen you and ordained you, that ye should go and bring forth fruit, and that your fruit should remain: that whatsoever ye shall ask of the Father in my name, he may give it you
17 These things I command you, that ye love one another.

Love

For him, [Rumi], although acknowledgedly one of the greatest poets of
Persia, poetry was only a secondary product. He did not regard it as any
more than a reflection of the enormous inner reality, which was truth, and
which, he calls love. The greatest love, as he says, is silent and cannot be
expressed in words.

Idries Shah,
The Sufis,
Garden City, N.Y., Anchor, 1971, p. 151

Query: When what we are doing is living out the commandment to
love, how do we respond to the query "What are you doing?" when we,
ourselves don't know where our actions fit in the will of God, only that
they are fruitful?

AUGUST 12

Romans 8:28

28 And we know that all things work [combine] together for good to
them that love God, to them who are called according to his purpose.

Love—Sacred and Profane

When the command to love God is accompanied by threats that God
will damn you to Hell forever with unceasing torture if you don't love
him, how can one respond? Here again men reveal the strange mixture
of anarchic power employed, with a vengeance, and human values that
are positive. It is humane individualism emerging from the anarchic
rugged individualism; it is the human being born out of the feral. It is
the gastronomic cycle being transfigured into human understanding and
cooperation.

When God is lovable, no command is necessary. To be sure while
feral man and feral god are undergoing transformation, the confusion
is great. When the process is complete we have the phenomenon of
Transfiguration.

Transfiguration from feral to human is not only a radical alteration
of outward appearance, a 'transformation of the figure'; it is above all a

radical internal change. Indeed, it is the internal that causes the external alteration.

In religious philosophy, it becomes clear that the transfigured feral man is accompanied by the transfigured feral god. As Xenophanes makes clear—the gods of Homer and Hesiod can no longer be gods for enlightened human beings (Xenophanes, for example!).

CEWLD

Query: How do we know that we love God? That we love one another? That we love ourselves?

AUGUST 13

Psalm 9:9

9 The LORD also will be a refuge for the oppressed, a refuge in times of trouble.

Stubborn

A stubborn person is one who insists on being his/her own person rather than what others say that he/she should be.

CEWLD

Query: Do the labels for tenacity vary in the definitions assigned by the labeler? Is it "stubbornness" when proven wrong and "steadfastness" when proven right?

AUGUST 14

Psalm 139:7–12

7 Whither shall I go from thy spirit? Or whither shall I flee from thy presence?
8 If I ascend up into heaven, thou art there: if I make my bed in hell, behold, thou art there.
9 If I take the wings of the morning, and dwell in the uttermost parts of the sea;

10 Even there shall thy hand lead me, and thy right hand shall hold me.
11 If I say, Surely the darkness shall cover me; even the night shall be light about me.
12 Yea, the darkness hideth not from thee: but the night shineth as the day: the darkness and the light are both alike to thee.

Credulity

The credulity of the human species at times seems utterly amazing, and crooks, commercial interests, propagandists (including the religious), and political 'leaders' have taken advantage of this tendency.

For some people, it is only necessary to hear a statement or to read it to evoke assent—it must be true. This is true not only of the people we like to describe as the untutored but also of people who have graduated from our professional schools and university graduate schools. There is an undue haste to believe something or to reject something because of a belief already fixed in the cerebral system.

A woman who should have known better was certain that the Communists had taken over Washington D.C., because the Democrats had won control of Congress. Moreover the Republican candidate for whom she had voted had lost to his Democrat opponent. A professor who was a recognized scholar in Hebrew, the Bible, and had a working knowledge of Arabic and Assyrian, knelt in his Baptist church and whined to God. His voice became that of a little child approaching a stern parent or of an Easterner groveling before an Oriental Despot. The same man could talk derisively of those who 'believed every word of the Bible, including the copyright.'

The mind of man so often seems to be schizoid, once he becomes literate and somewhat capable of realizing that he is able to believe or not believe.

We love absolutes; hence we are not satisfied with relative truths; ours must stand alone as absolutes. They are intolerant of competition.

We have too much confidence and faith in what we fail to grasp, and too little understanding of that which we are able to grasp.

Religion in its inclusive sense, would experience the totality of the Continuum of Occurrence, the drop of water wishes to swallow the ocean; the grain of sand, the mountain. This can be done only artistically by suggestion; hence all the rituals of religious organizations and the mysteries of the simple individual identifying him/herself with totality.

CEWLD

Query: Is that which we see merely what we "believe" that we see or does it exist on a spectrum independent of our perception? Does it matter to a life of service?

AUGUST 15

Psalm 19:2–4

2 Day unto day uttereth speech and night unto night sheweth knowledge.
3 There is no speech nor language where their voice is not heard.
4 Their line is gone out through all the earth and their words to the end of the world. In them hath he set a tabernacle for the sun.

Beautiful, The

His sense of the beautiful sets the human being apart from the lower animals. In brutes that sense is totally lacking. Man has no higher task than his endeavor to attain to this perfection, by some called Godlikeness. He has three means of approach in his progress toward this aim: Along the way of truth, the way of love, and the way that leads to beauty.

Rudolf F. Kung
Journal of Rifik ,
University of Nebraska, 1970, p. 187

Query: The Good, the True, the Beautiful, is one of the three within our field of vision, either inner or outer, as we read these words?

AUGUST 16

Psalms 104:24–27

24 O LORD, how manifold are thy works! in wisdom hast thou made them all: the earth is full of thy riches.
25 So is this great and wide sea, wherein are things creeping innumerable, both small and great beasts.
26 There go the ships: there is that leviathan, whom thou hast made to play therein.
27 These wait all upon thee; that thou givest them [that which] they gather: thou openest thine hand, they are filled with good.

Prosperity

What is bad? Too much? Too little? Moreover, the balance between the two is never attained with justice to all.

CEWLD

Query: Do we trust God in our economies as well as in our expenditures?

AUGUST 17

I Samuel 3:7–11

7 Now Samuel did not yet know the LORD, neither was the word of the LORD yet revealed unto him.
8 And the LORD called Samuel again the third time, And he arose and went to Eli, and said, Here am I; for thou didst call me. And Eli perceived that the LORD had called the child.
9 Therefore Eli said unto Samuel, Go, lie down: and it shall be, if he call thee, that thou shalt say, Speak, LORD; for thy servant heareth. So Samuel went and lay down in his place.
10 And the LORD came, and stood, and called as at other times, Samuel, Samuel. Then Samuel answered, Speak; for thy servant heareth.
11 And the LORD said to Samuel, Behold, I will do a thing in Israel, at which both the ears of every one that heareth it shall tingle.

Vocabularies

We speak and write and think in the vocabularies of individual experience. Words and thought structures of words are often identical to those employed by the other men and women of our society. The meanings, however, are often different. Thus we listen to someone or read what he has written; we are familiar with all the words and the ways in which they are put together. Yet we are puzzled and often ask, 'What does he mean?' 'What is she saying?'

CEWLD

Query: Do we use our reluctance to grasp a difficult and undifferentiated Calling to deny stepping into the unknown on faith? How much detail do we demand of God?

AUGUST 18

Mark 15:3

3 And the chief priests accused him of many things: but he answered nothing.

Virtue

Basic directions for becoming a martyr: Publicly uphold truth, decency, justice.
Note of encouragement: sometimes you can attain martyrdom by privately upholding human values.

CEWLD

Query: When a Power stands against Truth, how much truth do we speak to it?

AUGUST 19

Mark 9:36–37

36 For what shall it profit a man, if he gain the whole world, and lose his own soul?
37 Or what shall a man give in exchange for his soul?

Values

Since value is the driving force which is the source of human motivation, and hence of the formation of purposes, it is a vital factor in determining human action, and therefore also freedom. The whole course of human action throughout life is determined by values, economic, political, spiritual or legal.

Bronislaw Malinowski,
Freedom and Civilization,
University of Indiana, 1960, p. 131

Query: What is it that stings us so deeply tears spring to our eyes? What does this determine about our core values?

AUGUST 20

Psalm 113:9

9 He maketh the barren woman to keep house, and to be a joyful mother of children.

Certainty

Certainty shuts the door on everything but itself. Indeed, it desires to occupy total space and time. Historically, certainty has again and again rejected what is analytically true and what may be holistic truth.

CEWLD

Query: What can be rummaged for the future from an apparent end-of-the-line project, one which is seemingly barren of potentiality? Can we go forward by first going back?

AUGUST 21

Proverbs 4:1–13

1 Hear, ye children, the instruction of a father, and attend to know understanding.
2 For I give you good doctrine, forsake ye not my law.
3 For I was my father's son, tender and only beloved in the sight of my mother.
4 He taught me also, and said unto me, Let thine heart retain my word keep my commandments and live.
5 Get wisdom, get understanding: forget it not: neither decline from the words of my mouth.
6 Forsake her not, and she shall preserve thee: love her, and she shall keep thee.
7 Wisdom is the principle thing; therefore get wisdom: and with all thy getting get understanding.

8 Exalt her, and she shall promote thee: she shall bring thee to honour, when thou dost embrace her.
9 She shall give to thine head an ornament of grace: a crown of glory shall she deliver to thee.
10 Hear, O my son, and receive my sayings; and the years of thy life shall be many.
11 I have taught thee in the way of wisdom; I have led thee in right paths.
12 When thou goest, thy steps shall not be straitened; and when thou runnest, thou shalt not stumble.
13 Take fast hold of instruction; let her not go: keep her for she is thy life.

Teachers and Scholars

1. Scholars are given a form of permanence in print. Even if they do not attract the favorable attention of their fellow scholars, they tend to survive in the museum parts of university libraries.
2. Teachers have less permanence unless they are teacher-scholars whose thoughts are in print. The teacher reaches a far greater number of people than the scholar because of the almost endless flow of students passing before him during a teaching career lasting from, say, 25 years to 50. While the scholar knows pretty well what the judgment of his work is, the teacher can never know finally how broad or how tiny the influence wielded. Besides, how do we judge or can we judge the public school teacher who helps the student to become a person, a real independent human being? How does one rank the teacher who helps students to attain the status of confident adult? How can we trace the work of teachers who have not simply been concerned with information-gathering but have taught students "to think?" Is there any course called "How to think?" Yet the effective teacher, no matter what the subject matter, guides the student into thinking independently.

What is the "permanence" of such instruction? It cannot be measured or tallied in any respect. There is no way of testing a teacher-scholar so that we can say positively "Ms ABC teaches her students to think for themselves, and they become better students." Sometimes not even the students realize what Ms ABC has done for them until years later (if ever).

Spectacular teaching is recognized; great, effective teaching often passes unnoticed.

CEWLD

Query: Of Ruth and Naomi, who was the teacher and who the learner? Or perhaps was it alternating? Or simultaneous?

AUGUST 22

Deuteronomy 10:21

21 He is thy praise and he is thy God that hath done for thee these great and terrible things, which thine eyes have seen.

Questions—The Right

We tend to report favorably on those who ask the 'right' questions and to reprehend those who fail to do so. In both instances, of course, we are able to demonstrate our own superiority.

CEWLD

Query: Is it right to question God?

AUGUST 23

Proverbs 8:8–9

8 All the words of my mouth are in righteousness; there is nothing froward or perverse in them.
9 They are all plain to him that understandeth, and right to them that find knowledge.

Understanding

Even in the home of individual orientation, Europe and America, there is great confusion, most people living in a confusion of group-centeredness and individualism. [Note: Individual orientation has been coming into being during the last 2500 and more years. Whether it can come to fulfillment is still not clear. It may be killed by overpopulation and the economic straitjacket into which all people may be forced.]

CEWLD

Query: In following our Calling, where do we find our checks and balances to avoid distortions and deceptions?

AUGUST 24

Isaiah 5:17–21, 23

17 Then shall the lambs feed after their manner, and the waste places of the fat ones shall strangers eat.
18 Woe unto them that draw iniquity with cords of vanity, and sin as it were with a cart rope.
19 That say, Let him make speed, and hasten his work, that we may see it; and let the counsel of the Holy One of Israel draw nigh and come that we may know it!
20 Woe unto them that call evil good, and good evil; that put darkness for light, and light for darkness; that put bitter for sweet, and sweet for bitter!
21 Woe unto them that are wise in their own eyes, and prudent in their own sight!
23 Which justify the wicked for reward and take away the righteousness of the righteous from him!

Wisdom

Wisdom cries aloud in the streets; in the markets she raises her voice; on the top of the walls she cries out; at the entrance of the city gates she speaks, 'How long O simple ones, will you love being simple…?'

Proverbs 1:20–22 (RSV)

CEWLD

Query: Where is the voice of wisdom heard?

AUGUST 25

I Corinthians 1:26–27

26 For ye see your calling, brethren, how that not many wise men after the flesh, not many mighty, not many noble, are called:
27 But God hath chosen the foolish things of the world to confound the wise: and God hath chosen the weak things of the world to confound the things which are mighty.

Courage

Those must be regarded as most courageous who realize clearly what they face, yet do not shrink from danger.

Pericles [Quoted by Thucydides]

Query: Can we find courage to mind our Calling in domestic situations? Under social pressure? When survival is at stake?

AUGUST 26

Job 22:1–14 [Words of Eliphaz: Job has sinned and merits his punishment.]

1 Then Eliphaz the Temanite answered and said.
2 Can a man be profitable unto God, as he that is wise may be profitable unto himself?
3 Is it any pleasure to the Almighty that thou art righteous? Or is it gain to him that thou makest thy ways perfect?
4 Will he reprove thee for fear of thee? Will he enter with thee into judgment?
5 Is not thy wickedness great? And thine iniquities infinite?
6 For thou hast taken a pledge from thy brother for nought, and stripped the naked of their clothing.
7 Thou hast not given water to the weary to drink, and thou hast withholden bread from the hungry.
8 But as for the mighty man, he had the earth; and the honourable man dwelt in it.
9 Thou hast sent widows away empty, and the arms of the fatherless have been broken.
10 Therefore snares are round about thee, and sudden fear troubleth thee;
11 Or darkness, that thou canst not see; and abundance of waters cover thee.
12 Is not God in the height of heaven? And behold the height of the stars how high they are!
13 And thou sayest, How doth God know? Can he judge through the dark cloud?
14 Thick clouds are a covering to him that he seeth not; and he walketh in the circuit of heaven.

Emptying Oneself

Knowledge is speech at its most impersonal, its most objective. Man can face up to the truth; he can try to empty himself of all his preconceptions and see things—some things—as they are. In this way he comes to know a world which transcends the limitations of his own life. This is the great attraction of the theoretic life.

Karl Britton,
Philosophy and the Meaning of Life,
Cambridge University Press, 1969, p. 68

Query: How is the Voice recognized that speaks into the emptied self? Or does it rise from within and simply become audible when all else is silenced?

AUGUST 27

Matthew 7:21

21 Not every one that saith unto me Lord, Lord, shall enter into the kingdom of heaven; but he that doeth the will of my Father which is in heaven.

Lord, Lord,

… the translators and editors of the Bible (OT, RSV, 1952) deliberately adapted the material to reflect contemporary viewpoints. In a scholarly translation of the Bible, we would hope to approach the source material as closely as possible. (I say "source material" because there are no originals.) In reading the 1611 translation, often called the 'King James Version', we have the Bible more or less unwittingly … reflecting the Elizabethan culture; in the 1952, the contemporary concepts are deliberately introduced.

It is doubtful if a meticulously translated and edited scholarly edition of the Bible will ever be possible. It is not commercially possible and no one is likely to pay out a great deal of money on behalf of pure scholarship.

People who do not know Hebrew, Greek, Latin, Aramaic, Arabic, Syriac, Akkadian, Sumerian, Egyptian, Coptic, Ethiopian, Hittite,

Canaanite, Moabite, Edomite and a dozen or so other languages will have to make do with what is available!

CEWLD

Query: Does one ever address the LORD with an imperative sentence in prayer…as in "Just do…" or "God bless" (as in God bless America)?

AUGUST 28

Exodus 32:18–19

18 And he said, It is not the voice of them that shout for mastery, neither is it the voice of them that cry for being overcome: but the noise of them that sing do I hear.
19 And it came to pass, as soon as he came nigh unto the camp, that he saw the calf, and the dancing: and Moses' anger waxed hot, and he cast the tables [stone tablets of the Ten Commandments] out of his hand and brake them beneath the mount [Sinai].

Mastery

If one cannot master the parts without understanding the whole and cannot understand the whole without comprehending the parts, what can one ever master? The only conclusion permitted us is that no one finally masters anything. Some go so far beyond the others that they seem to have reached the goal, but this is only an illusion of perspective.

CEWLD

Query: In seeking security, how much of the responsibility for worldly or heavenly understanding do we delegate to others in the regulation of our days?

AUGUST 29

Hebrews 11:15–16

15 And truly, if they had been mindful of that country from whence they came out, they might have had opportunity to have returned.

16 But now they desire a better country, that is, an heavenly: wherefore God is not ashamed to be called their God for he hath prepared for them a city.

Lord, LORD

Those people who resent college courses entitled 'The Bible as Literature' are apparently ignorant of the whole matter of translation. Insofar as the Bible is edited so as to support contemporary religious concepts, it is literature!

CEWLD

Query: Can we understand the answers without living the questions?

AUGUST 30

Luke 6:34–38

34 And if ye lend to them of whom ye hope to receive, what thank have ye? For sinners also lend to sinners, to receive as much again.
35 But love ye your enemies, and do good, and lend, hoping for nothing again; and your reward shall be great, and ye shall be the children of the Highest: for he is kind unto the unthankful and to the evil.
36 Be ye therefore merciful, as your Father also is merciful.
37 Judge not, and ye shall not be judged: condemn not, and ye shall not be condemned: forgive, and ye shall be forgiven:
38 Give, and it shall be given unto you: good measure, pressed down, and shaken together, and running over, shall men give into your bosom. For with the same measure that ye mete, withal shall it be measured unto you again.

Evil and the Power of Good

Disinteredness and active kindness wield an extraordinary influence over men's minds and are the sources of a curious kind of non-compulsive power. In the first fifty years of their existence the Capuchins had thoroughly earned this power and influence. It is one of the tragedies of history that this moral force should everywhere have been exploited, by the rulers of the Church and State, for the furtherance of their own generally sinister ends. This harnessing by evil of the power generated by goodness is one of the principal and most tragic themes of human history.

Aldous Huxley
Grey Eminence,
New York, Chatto Windus, 1956, p. 42

Query: Is the lesser of two evils still evil? Is there a third choice?

AUGUST 31

Proverbs 30:18–19

18 There are three things which are too wonderful for me, yea, four which I know not:
19 The way of an eagle in the air; the way of a serpent upon a rock; the way of a ship in the midst of the sea; and the way of a man with a maid.

Creative Solutions

I think it is in *The Way Things Are* that Percy Bridgman told of discovering in his dreams how to set up an apparatus. The biologist Szent-Gyogyi dreamed conclusions. So too Bertrand Russell (*Autobiography*) had results flash into consciousness. In my discussions of thinking, I have described this phenomenon in terms of permutations and combinations performed in the 'mind' with conscious effort.

CEWLD

Query: Does a dream show us our "heart" as "As a man thinketh in his heart, so is he"? Does inspiration come from heart-knowledge or from head-knowledge—or indeed from something "breathed in" from outside one's ken?

☙September☙

SEPTEMBER 1

I Peter 5:5–6

5 Likewise ye younger, submit yourselves unto the elder. Yea, all of you be subject one to another, and be clothed with humility: for God resisteth the proud, and giveth grace to the humble.
6 Humble yourselves therefore under the mighty hand of God, that he may exalt you in due time.

Yourself

From time to time you have no alternative but to fall back on yourself, your own powers, your own capacities be they great or small. The older you become, the more that death removes family and friends, the more alone you will be. Then comes the testing time, whether you can endure being so very much alone, whether your pride will prevent your revealing your sense of isolation, whether you have anything to fall back upon, whether you 'can take it.'

The scene changes constantly and visibly, but other changes are not equally manifest. On this or that occasion you become aware of the fact that you no longer fit into the world. You are a piece from a game that was completed some time ago. You do not belong. Have you the strength to take it? Will you break out in wrath against younger people and make them unhappy enough to wish that you were long since dead? Or will you somehow manage to live on your own resources whatever they may be? *Dass das Leben schwer ist weiss man; Dass es unerträglich ist weiss man nicht—Gott sei dank!* [That life is difficult, one knows; that life is unbearable, one does not know…thank God!]

Sometimes it seems that the so-called Powers of the Universe desire to see 'how much a person can take' before he admits that he is beaten, or before death stops the game.

How can you 'be yourself' when all the forces of human existence have worked to shape you into something other than 'yourself'?

CEWLD

Query: How do we bring the isolated into friendship? Into community?

SEPTEMBER 2

Psalm 31:21–22

21 Blessed be the LORD: for he hath shewed me his marvelous kindness in a strong city.
22 For I said in my haste, I am cut off from before thine eye nevertheless thou heardest the voice of my supplications when I cried unto thee.

Appearances

Romans 2:11

11 For there is no respect of persons with God. [KJV]
11 For God shows no partiality. [RSV]

Latin: *non enim est personarum acceptio apud Deum.*
Swedish: *Ty hos Gud ar intet anfsende till person* [handwritten Swedish].

The English translations are wholly inadequate. The sense of the verse is that God, unlike a lot of human beings, does not judge people on the basis of appearance alone. No matter what an appealing appearance a person offers, this is not enough. This is a jab at the rest of us who are impressed by what is on the surface. Paul is really saying, 'God ain't like that—he respects (or judges on the basis of) what you really are.'

CEWLD

Query: If you could see the totality of love God has for another human being, how would that change your life? What if that person was an outcast or became one?

SEPTEMBER 3

Proverbs 28:18-21

18 Whoso walketh uprightly shall be saved: but he that is perverse in his ways shall fall at once.

19 He that tilleth his land shall have plenty of bread: but he that followeth after vain persons shall have poverty enough.

20 A faithful man shall abound with blessing but he that maketh haste to be rich shall not be innocent.

21 To have respect of persons is not good: for, for a piece of bread that man will transgress.

Purity Codes

The ideas of taboo became transformed into the ideas of purity and impurity when they were associated with a belief in the gods. Above all else the gods demand purity in those who approach them.

Martin P. Nilsson,
A History of Greek Religion, 2nd ed. Rev. (1952)
New York, Norton, 1964, p. 82

Query: Who is pure enough to pray without fear, without an interpreter, without an anointed intermediary?

SEPTEMBER 4

Mark 2:14–17

14 And as he passed by he saw Levi the son of Alphaeus sitting at the receipt of custom, and said unto him, follow me. And he arose and followed him.

15 And it came to pass, that as Jesus sat at meat in his house, many publicans and sinners sat also together with Jesus and his disciples, for there were many, and they followed him.

16 And when the scribes and Pharisees saw him eat with publicans and sinners they said unto his disciples, How is it that he eateth and drinketh with publicans and sinners?

17 When Jesus heard it, he saith unto them, They that are whole have no need of the physician, but they that are sick; I came not to call the righteous, but sinners to repentance.

Fragmentation

Strictly speaking, I can have no knowledge of God except such as I derive from the limited vision of my secondary perceptions on this single planet. Such knowledge is a fragment of a fragment.

Goethe
Cited by Will and Ariel Durant,
Rousseau and Revolution,
New York, Simon and Schuster,1967, p. 620
[The Durants cite their source as Lewisohn, *Goethe, II*, p. 210}

Query: We wait for instruction ... how long? When action is urgent ... how long? Instruction from whence?

SEPTEMBER 5

Isaiah 26:1

1 In that day shall this song be sung in the land of Judah; We have a strong city; salvation will God appoint for walls and bulwarks.

Fragmentation

I knew that one's life, one's spanning of years and places, could never be of a piece, but rather were like scattered fragments of old glass.

Willie Morris,
North Toward Home,
New York, Dell, 1970, pp. 382–383

Query: Looking back, looking ahead, where does one step across the present from one to the other?

SEPTEMBER 6

Song of Solomon 8:5–7

5 Who is this that cometh up from the wilderness, leaning upon her beloved? I raised thee up under the apple tree: there thy mother brought thee forth: there she brought thee forth that bare thee.

6 Set me as a seal upon thine heart, as a seal upon thine arm: for love is strong as death: jealousy is cruel as the grave: the coals thereof are coals of fire, which hath a most vehement flame.
7 Many waters cannot quench love, neither can the floods drown it: if a man would give all the substance of his house for love, it would utterly be condemned.

Fragmentation

Of that which constitutes our inner life we can import to even to those most intimate with us only fragments; the whole of it we cannot give, nor would they be able to comprehend it.

Albert Schweitzer,
Memoirs of Childhood and Youth,
New York, Macmillan, 1963, p. 109

Query: How deeply into our inner life can we accept the intimate contact of another soul?

SEPTEMBER 7

Micah 5:2

2 But thou, Beth-lehem Ephratah [Fruitful House of Bread], though thou be little among the thousands of Judah, yet out of thee shall he come forth unto me that is to be ruler in Israel; whose goings forth have been from of old, from everlasting.

The Past

My life as I lived it had often seemed to me like a story that has no beginning and no end. I had the feeling that I was a historical fragment, an excerpt for which the preceding and succeeding text was missing. My life seemed to have been snipped out of a long chain of events, and many questions had remained unanswered.

C. G. Jung
Memories, Dreams, Reflections,
New York, Vintage, 1965, p. 193

Query: How can the past be changed?

SEPTEMBER 8

Romans 16:19

19 For your obedience is come abroad unto all men. I am glad therefore on your behalf: but yet I would have you wise unto that which is good and simple concerning evil.

Fragmentarian

The concepts we create, the laws we find, are fragments in the whole language of nature. The marvel is that we get along so well when we speak so little of her language: when we guess only parts of the vocabulary, and few of the grammatical rules which connect them.

J. Bronowski,
The Identity of Man,
Garden City, New York,
Doubleday, Natural History Press, 1971, p. 41

Query: What is the language of the dawn? The voice in the earthquake? The murmur in the silence after each?

SEPTEMBER 9

Genesis 8:22

22 While the earth remaineth, seedtime and harvest, and cold and heat and summer and winter, and day and night shall not cease.

Fragmentation and Wholeness

Although the primal unity can only be experienced fragmentarily, it has at least come within range of conscious experience, whereas for the undeveloped ego it was utterly overwhelming.

Erich Neumann
Origins and History of Consciousness,

Princeton, 1971, p. 329

Query: The dream of the tidal wave, what does it represent?

SEPTEMBER 10

Deuteronomy 28:2–3

2 And all these blessings shall come on thee, and overtake thee, if thou shalt hearken unto the voice of the LORD thy God.
3 Blessed shalt thou be in the city, and blessed shalt thou be in the field.

Youth Regained

[Utnapishtim reveals to Gilgamesh in secret — a plant growing under water that restores youth. Gilgamesh finds it.]

Gilgamesh said to Urshanabi, the ferryman, 'Come here and see this marvelous plant. By its virtue a man may win back all his former strength. I will take it to Uruk of the Strong Walls; there I will give it to the old man to eat. Its name shall be "The Old Men are Young Again"; and at last I shall eat it myself and have back all my lost youth.'

N. K. Sanders,
The Epic of Gilgamesh, (1969, rev. 1964, rev. 1972)
Baltimore, Penguin, 1973, p. 116

Query: Are there yet ways in which the past may be changed or the effects of the past constrained?

SEPTEMBER 11

II Chronicles 15:7

7 Be ye strong therefore, and let not your hands be weak; for your work shall be rewarded.

Fragmentation

When you are still fragmented, lacking certainty—what difference does it make what your decisions are?

Hakim Sanai,
The Walled Garden of Truth,
Cited by Idries Shah, *The Sufis*,
Garden City, N.Y., Anchor, 1971, p. 245

Query: When the reward comes, why is it often a surprise though won many times over?

SEPTEMBER 12

Exodus 33:13–14

13 Now therefore I pray thee, if I have found grace in thy sight, shew me now thy way, that I may know thee, that I may find grace in thy sight: and consider that this nation is thy people.
14 And he said, My presence shall go with thee, and I will give thee rest.

Hasidim

The core of Hasidic faith was said to consist in their belief that the presence of God permeates and sustains all living matter and in the intense enthusiasm that they impart to their every action. (The Hebrew word 'hasidim' means 'pious ones'—those who are especially dedicated to fulfilling the divinely appointed laws.) The scope of Hasidic devotion extended to all aspects of life, infusing holiness in work, in eating, and in social intercourse.

J.K.Mintz,
Legends of the Hasidim (1968),
University of Chicago, 1974, p. 26

Query: Do we allow the privileges of the scholar, the celebrant, the holy, fully to women? To ourselves?

SEPTEMBER 13

Deuteronomy 28:2–3

2 And all these blessings shall come on thee, and overtake thee, if thou shalt hearken unto the voice of the LORD thy God.
3 Blessed shalt thou be in the city, and blessed shalt thou be in the field.

Freedom

For primitive people, everything was sacred. It took civilization to provide experiences of free and not free.

CEWLD

Query: Is freedom a quality which exists on a sliding scale?

SEPTEMBER 14

Proverbs 16:32

32 He that is slow to anger is better than the mighty and he that ruleth his spirit than he that taketh a city.

Rule

'What,' he [Confucius] asked, 'has one who is not able to govern himself to do with governing others?'

Elias Canetti,
Crowds and Power,
New York, Compass, 1966, p. 210

Query: If one is waiting for our wisdom/advice and comes upon us suddenly for it, what is our inner response?

SEPTEMBER 15

II Chronicles: 32:20–21

20 And thus did Hezekiah throughout all Judah, and wrought that which was good and right and truth before the LORD his God.
21 And in every work that he began in the service of the house of God, and in the law and in the commandments, to seek his God, he did it with

all his heart, and prospered.

Word—No Word For It

[New Guinea, Father Fisker, S.V.D., of the mission at Gumine]

But it is not easy. Even after you learn their language well, you find that they do not even have words to express some of the basic things we try to teach, very few words to indicate abstractions. For example, they have no word for 'hope' and there is no word for 'love.' How can we teach Christian ideas without these two words? The closest approach to the word love is the phrase 'I do good to you.' It is not the same, of course, but it gets across at least one part of the idea of loving.

Lewis Cotlow,
In Search of the Primitive,
Little, Brown & G., 1966, p. 344.

Query: When a door with no name opens before us, how do we know to go through it?

SEPTEMBER 16

Isaiah 27:1–6

1 In that day the LORD with his sore and great and strong sword, shall punish leviathan the piercing serpent, even leviathan that crooked serpent; and he shall slay the dragon that is in the sea.
2 In that day, sing ye unto her, A vineyard of red wine.
3 I the LORD do keep it; I will water it every moment: lest any hurt it, I will keep it night and day.
4 Fury is not in me: who would set the briers and thorns against me in battle? I would go through them, I would burn them together.
5 Or let him take hold of my strength, that he may make peace with me; and he shall make peace with me.
6 He shall cause them that come of Jacob to take root: Israel shall blossom and bud, and fill the face of the world with fruit.

Word—No Word For It—2

When the European fire chariots were first run upon their iron roads, as the Chinese phrase it, it had become necessary to coin words for everything connected with them. So a railway platform was oddly dubbed a 'moon-viewing verandah'; nothing nearer to it, in the Chinese world, could be thought of.

George N. Kates,
The Years That Were Fat: The Last of Old China, (1952)
Cambridge, Mass., MIT, 1967, p. 9

Query: Can we find meaning when we have no word to describe what we've found?

SEPTEMBER 17

Psalm 94:17

17 Unless the LORD had been my help, my soul had almost dwelt in silence.

Absolutism—Religion

To believe that one has attained absolute truth in his religious faith is to flirt with untruth.

The believer in the absolute will be challenged and his defense will invariably lead him into rationalizing. Rationalizing is invariably dishonest, and the rationalizer at last becomes one who warps the truth. Philosophical (and theological) rationalizers have enjoyed considerable success because they mix the holistic and the analytical, the logical and the irrational.

The safest course for the absolutists in religion is that adopted by the believer who wishes no defense, who simply says, 'I believe,' and that is the sum total of his (her) position.

CEWLD

Query: Does God's Truth require human defenders?

SEPTEMBER 18

Psalm 25:4–5

4 Show me thy ways, O, LORD; teach me thy paths.
5 Lead me in thy truth, and teach me: for thou art the God of my
salvation; on thee do I wait all the day.

Decisions and Free Will:

To make a decision is to exercise free will. The quality and the extent of
free will is determined by the quality and extent of decisions, with quality
of major importance. If one is allowed to make all minor decisions
but no major decisions, free will is greatly impaired and may approach
zero in value. If one makes major decisions, free will is greatly enriched.
Furthermore the right to make minor decisions is taken for granted. Note
that none of us is able to decide the following: (1) whether or not we
shall be biologically conceived; (2) to what parents in what location, at
what time the conception will occur; (3) whether the conception will go
full term; (4) what the gene complex will be; (5) what the environments
(prenatal and postnatal will be.

Note also that in group-centered societies many of the most important
decisions are not permitted. In certain ethnic groups, one does not,
himself or herself, select a matrimonial mate.

Note also that decisions are closely tied in with the economic
factors. Our predecessors in mini-societies of pre-civilized ages had
few opportunities to exercise free will ... so busy were they in surviving
biologically. We are presently moving toward the opposite situation of
macro-societies, of limitations of space, of biological overcrowding in the
earth.

Decision-making and free will are tied in with the socio-economic
circumstances that we deliberately, and also unawaredly, create.

I. Mini-societies Food gathering; hunting
II. Meso-societies Poleis, city-states, nomadic tribes
III. Macro-societies Egypt, Rome, China, the USA, Russia, Japan,
Europe, Brazil

Query: Can the Leading from God come from the words of a friend? A
mentor? A civic leader? How do those words reach the heart to bear fruit?
Is there "civic inspiration"?

SEPTEMBER 19

I Timothy 1:5

5 Now the end of the commandment is charity [love] out of a pure heart, and of a good conscience, and of faith unfeigned.

Self

In the past the self had garments, the garments of station, of nobility or inferiority, and each self had its carriage, its looks, wore the sheath appropriate to it. Now there were no sheaths and it was naked self with naked self burning intolerably and causing terror. I saw this now, in a fit of objectivity.

[Charles Citrine speaking—the main *dramatis persona*.]
Saul Bellow,
Humbolt's Gift, (1973, 74, 75)
New York, Avon, 1976, p. 213

Query: When I say "I", is the same person speaking who spoke yesterday? Who will speak tomorrow?

SEPTEMBER 20

Proverbs 3:25–27

25 Be not afraid of sudden fear, neither of the desolation of the wicked, when it cometh.
26 For the LORD shall be thy confidence, and shall keep thy foot from being taken.
27 Withhold not good from them to whom it is due, when it is in the power of thine hand to do it.

Decisions

Insofar as we ask other people to make decisions regarding what we should do and say, we are not mature. Nor can we be moral or immoral. A robot, well programmed, may make excellent decisions in the area for which it has been adjusted, but those are not the robot's own decisions. A computing machine is not a human being but a human product.

To decide personally is to assume personal responsibility. To parrot some one else is to take up responsibility for that other person's decisions.

In other words to use the decisions of others is to be either a beneficiary or a victim of someone else's solution to a given problem.

CEWLD

Query: Even in a determinist world with few choices left to the individual, can we act as though all choices were free in the chance that the pivotal one(s) in which we are truly free will be made boldly and correctly…with confidence?

SEPTEMBER 21

Psalm 91:1

1 He that dwelleth in the secret places of the most High shall abide under the shadow of the Almighty.

Strangers and Clients

From time to time it has occurred to me that professional people have very little knowledge of the people who are their clients, patients, customers, or whatever else. It takes time to build up a human rapport between the professional and the person employing his services; it also takes talk, conversation. But there is no time for talk; time is money. Years ago I knew a physician and surgeon with an intimacy that nowadays often fills me with wonder. We did not meet often, but the encounters were natural and human. So too, the brief conversations touched always our humanity. Since WWII, I have been here in the "friendly" west. In a couple of months it will be 27 years that I have been in Portland. I have had these, almost 27 years, dealings with one bank. Off and on, I have had dealings for 25 years with one law firm. I have encountered any number of physicians.

   Most of the people know almost nothing about me beyond services rendered. There is no time. I have recognized the human touch in two or three in the medical profession, but no one has much time. We are all on the assembly line. Not only is the personal touch gone, but with it a human knowledge for which there is no substitute.

CEWLD

Query: What does one do with a sudden intimate understanding of the condition of another person?

SEPTEMBER 22

II Samuel 8:28

28 And now, O Lord GOD, thou art that God, and thy words be true, and thou hast promised this goodness unto thy servant:

Pioneer

It is only too easy to reproach a pioneer for having strayed off the track—but the track did not exist when he began his work.

C.W.Ceram,
The Secret of the Hittites, (1955),
New York, Schocken, 1973, pp. 96–97

Query: Can we see blessings on the unlighted paths in difficult times?

SEPTEMBER 23

Mark 11:29–30

29 And Jesus answered and said unto them, I will also ask of you one question, and answer me, and I will tell you by what authority I do these things.
30 The baptism of John, was it from heaven, of men? Answer me.

Questions, Reporter's Standard

Trite phrases notwithstanding, human nature does change, so the historian must be slow to read into another age the motivations of his own—even the surfacing of biological urges triggered by the cultural environment as they may be. To answer Who, What, When, Where and How, the first five of the reporter's standard questions is much easier than to tell [the sixth], Why, not alone because the five questions must be answered before the sixth can be raised.

Robin W. Winks,
The Historian as Detective,
(1968, 1969), edited by Robin W. Winks,
New York, Harper & Row, 1970, p. 279

Query: When we speak with authority, do others hear it and perceive from whence it came?

SEPTEMBER 24

I Corinthians 1:26

26 For ye see your calling, brethren, how that not many wise men after the flesh, not many mighty, not many noble, are called:

Conditioning

Men trained in a profession come by degrees into the profession's channel, and flow only in one direction, and always between the same banks. The master of a learned profession at last becomes its slave. He is a soul of that calling's shape.

David Swing,
Cited by Cassius J. Keyser,
Mathematical Philosophy: A Study of Fate and Freedom,
New York, E.P. Dutton, 1922, p. 453

Query: When does our channel become a rut? A prison?

SEPTEMBER 25

I Chronicles 29:14

14 But who am I, and what is my people, that we should be able to offer so willingly after this sort? For all things come of thee, and of thine own have we given thee.
15 For we are strangers before thee, and sojourners, as were all our fathers, our days on the earth are as a shadow, and there is none abiding.

Beautiful, The

For beauty is not perfection of form and color, but the expression of indwelling spirit, i.e. of the soul.

Rudolf F. Kurz,
Journal of RFK,
University of Nebraska, 1970, p. 272

Query: Can we perceive the beauty that looks back on us no matter what face it wears?

SEPTEMBER 26

Ecclesiastes 4:9–10

9 Two are better than one because they have a good reward for their labour.
10 For if they fall, the one will lift up his fellow; but woe to him that is alone when he falleth; for he hath not another to help him up.

Sacred—Center as Zone of the Sacred

The center then, is pre-eminently the zone of the sacred, the zone of absolute reality. Similarly, all the other symbols of absolute reality (trees of life and immortality, Fountain of Youth, etc.) are also situated at the center. The road leading to the center is a difficult road ... and this is verified at every level of reality....

Mircea Eliade,
Cosmos and History: The Myth of the Eternal Return,
New York, Harper & Row, 1959, pp. 17–18

Query: Do we obey the Inner Voice despite appearances and despite the demurs of others?

SEPTEMBER 27

Proverbs 25:11

11 A word fitly spoken is like apples of gold in pictures of silver.

Reporters

A good reporter, if he chooses the right approach, can understand a cat or an Arab. The choice is the problem, and if he chooses [wrongly] he will come away scratched or baffled. (There is a different approach to every cat and every Arab.)

A.J. Liebling,
The Press, Second Edition, Revised
New York, Ballantine, 1975, p. 120

Query: Do we have a regard for posterity and legacy when we utter or write words of truth or is the utterance or writing of them simply commending them to God's hands and use?

SEPTEMBER 28

Isaiah 26:12

12 LORD, thou wilt ordain peace for us for thou also hast wrought all our works in us.

Sectarianism

Only the ... sectarian is in a position to embrace a religion in its fullness. The nonsectarian may not do this, but he/she is in a position to do so. The situation sometimes approaches the ludicrous. One may be a Christian who is a Roman Catholic, Orthodox, Protestant, or other; at the same time he may be a member of a sect within a sect and even a sect which is within a sect, which is within a sect. One is not just a Methodist, for example, or a Baptist, or a Lutheran; one is a particular kind of Methodist, Baptist, or Lutheran. Even in a particular community or parish, one will find foetal sects, which are never quite aborted and never quite born.

CEWLD

Query: Do the words and wisdom of others help us find peace with God?

SEPTEMBER 29

I Corinthians 14:25

25 And thus are the secrets of his heart made manifest; and so falling down upon his face he will worship God, and report that God is in you of a truth.

Marriage

The institution of sacred marriage must be as old in the Indo-European race as the domestic religions; for the one could not exist without the other. This religion taught man that the conjugal union was something more than a relation of the sexes and a fleeting affection, and united man and wife by the powerful bond of the same worship and the same belief. The marriage ceremony too, was so solemn, and produced effects so grave, that it is not surprising that these men did not think it [was] permitted or was possible to have more than one wife in each house. Such a religion could not admit of polygamy.

We can understand, too, that such a marriage was indissoluble, and that divorce was almost impossible....

Fustel de Coulanges (1830–1889),
The Ancient City (1864; tr. Engl. 1873),
Garden City, N.Y., Anchor, n.d. pp. 47–48

(Note: Fustel notes that the marriage could be dissolved by a solemn religious rite.)

CEWLD

Query: How do the indissoluble bonds between human beings relate to the secrets of the heart and to the will of God? Can we ever guarantee against error?

SEPTEMBER 30

I Corinthians 9:19–22

19 For though I be free from all men, yet have I made myself servant

unto all, that I might gain the more.

20 And unto the Jews I became as a Jew, that I might gain the Jews; to them that are under the law, as under the law, that I might gain them that are under the law;

21 To them that are without law, as without law, (being not without law to God, but under the law to Christ) that I might gain them that are without law.

22 To the weak became I as weak, that I might gain the weak: I am made all things to all men, that I might by all means save some.

Boundaries

Since a hero is created in the image of a people's ideals, he tends to be all things to all men.

Ivan Morris,
The Nobility of Failure [Japan], (1975),
New York, Meridian, 1976, p. 1

Query: How deeply can one merge with another before losing oneself? Is that loss desirable or dangerous? How deeply can one merge with the Holy? Can the Holy be distinguished from its reverse?

OCTOBER

OCTOBER 1

I Corinthians 14:40

40 Let all things be done decently and in order.

Order

Order is not a pressure, which is imposed on society from without, but an equilibrium, which is set up from within.

Oxford Dictionary of Quotations
Elizabeth Knowles, Ed.
Oxford University Press, 1971

Query: Where does the stranger fit into the order of a small community? How does a daughter-in-law show respect for her mother-in-law in religious tradition not her own—as in Ruth and Naomi in The Book of Ruth?

OCTOBER 2

Psalm 127:1

1 Except the LORD build the house, they labour in vain that build it: except the LORD keep the city, the watchman waketh but in vain.

City, Ancient

What we have already seen of ancient institutions and above all of ancient beliefs has enabled us to obtain an idea of the profound gulf, which always separated two cities. However near to each other they might be, they always formed two completely separate societies. Between them there was much more than the distance, which separates two cities today, much more than the frontier, which separates two states; their gods were not the same or their ceremonies, or their prayers. The worship of one city was forbidden to men of a neighboring city. The belief was, that the gods of one city rejected the homage and prayers of any one who was not their own citizen.

These ancient beliefs, it is true, were modified and softened in the course of time; but they had been in their full vigor at the time when these societies were formed, and these societies always preserved the impression of them.

Numa Deus Fustel de Coulanges,
The Ancient City, (1864; Engl. Tr.1873)
Garden City, N.Y., Anchor, n.d., p. 201

Query: Does worship within a denomination which is strange to us still give us access through prayer to the same deity?

OCTOBER 3

Psalm 24:26

26 The meek shall eat and be satisfied: they shall praise the LORD that seek him: and your heart shall live forever.

City, Ancient

There was not a single act of public life in which the gods were not seen to take a part. As he was under the influence of the idea that they were by turns excellent protectors or cruel enemies, man never dared to act without being sure that they were favorable.

Numa Deus Fustel de Coulanges,
The Ancient City (1864; Eng. Tr. 1873),
Garden City, N.Y., Anchor, n.d., p. 201

Query: How best to please God, follow good or flee evil?

OCTOBER 4

Philippians 1:25

25 And having this confidence, I know that I shall abide and continue with you all for your furtherance and joy of faith.

City, Ancient

The ancient city was really the sacred center, the fortress of the community. Each citizen actually lived on his own land apart from the center.

CEWLD

For several generations yet, men continued to live outside the city, in isolated families that divided the soil among them. Each of these families occupied its canton, where it had its domestic sanctuary, and where it formed, under the authority of its *pater*, an indivisible group.

Numa Deus Fustel de Coulanges,
The Ancient City (1864; Eng. Tr. 1873),
Garden City, N.Y., Anchor, n.d., p. 229

Query: Do we trust our place in the Heavenly City or do we prefer our place in the cathedral of nature's beauty? Are these views of Paradise mutually exclusive?

OCTOBER 5

Micah 4:6–7

6 In that day, saith the LORD, will I assemble her that halteth, and I will gather her that is driven out, and her that I have afflicted;
7 And I will make her that was cast far off a strong nation: and the LORD shall reign over them in mount Zion from henceforth, even forever.

Hero

In the mystique of Japanese heroism nothing succeeds like failure.

Ivan Morris,
The Nobility of Failure [Japan], (1975),
New York, Meridian, 1976, p. 15

Query: Are we aware of the turning point after long perseverance? Does our awareness matter?

OCTOBER 6

Romans 4:20–22

20 He staggered not at the promise of God through unbelief; but was strong in faith, giving glory to God;
21 And being fully persuaded that what he had promised, he was able to perform.
22 And therefore it was imputed to him for righteousness.

Faith

Faith is static. It claims to grasp the absolute; hence it cannot be creative. Anyone who has grasped the absolute, the all-in-all, is through. Such a person has all the answers, knows all the rules of life and Being (if there are any rules for the Absolute!), and has nothing to do but to remain in absolute....

In other words, human beings were conditioned to belief, to have faith in something. So powerful was this conditioning that scientists and other thinkers, considering themselves atheists, simply transferred their faith from religion to science. It is almost pathetic to observe how 19th century scientists and many also of the 20th century scientists did not abandon faith and certitude; they simply took them out of religion and placed them in science. They also congratulated themselves and their fellow specialists that they were no longer imprisoned in faith, that is, religious faith.

CEWLD

Query: How much is the faith that is ours unique to us in its expression? How many paths of faith are acceptable to God?

OCTOBER 7

I Peter 2:17

17 Honour all men. Love the brotherhood. Fear God. Honour the king.

Example

For, whenever the chiefs of the state deem anything honourable, the other citizens are sure to follow their example....

"Aristotle's Politics, Book II, Chap. II."
Aristotle's Politics and Poetics,
Tr. Berg, Jowett and Thomas, Twining (1952),
New York, Viking, 1957. p. 54

Children are educated by what the grownup is, and not by what he says.

C.G. Jung,
Essays on the Science of Mythology,
Princeton, N.J., Bollingen, 1969, p. 94

We are always disappointed in 'other people' when they fail to be the good and reliable examples that society always desperately needs.

CEWLD

Query: Are we aware when others feel we have failed their expectations? Does it matter?

OCTOBER 8

Proverbs 3:2–4

2 For length of days and long life, and peace, shall they add to thee.
3 Let not mercy and truth forsake thee: bind them about thy neck; write them upon the table of thine heart:
4 So shalt thou find favour and good understanding in the sight of God and man.

World, Personal

Most of us live in a personal world of our own imagination. What the actual world is at large—physical, social, intellectual, religious, artistic, etc.—nobody fully knows, and no one can define it or adequately describe it.

Some of the personal worlds seem to fit into the 'rest of the world' so neatly, that an individual feels wholly adapted to whatever is, and, if he stops to think at all, is convinced that he is in touch with reality. Other personal worlds, however, are colliding with 'other worlds', with the consequence that the victims of the collisions become reformers, rebels, or emotionally disturbed people, often very unhappy people.

As long as everything occurs with little or no understanding — no enlightenment — society will remain somewhat disordered, and the reactions will be, for the most part, emotional, often enough unintelligent.

To some extent a full-fledged artist creates his world out of his experiences and emotionally, at least, substitutes it for all other worlds. It is still, however, an imaginary world, no matter how much it illuminates other 'worlds.'

CEWLD

Query: How may we simplify our communication so as to extend our words to reach across interpersonal boundaries of the individual's personal world(s)?

OCTOBER 9

Psalm 140:8

8 Cause me to hear thy lovingkindness in the morning; for in thee do I trust: cause me to know the way wherein I should walk; for I lift up my soul to thee.

Poor

Generally my fellow townspeople, though they would help the poor, were not particularly fond of them.

Elie Wiesel,
Night (1958),
New York, Avon, 1969, p. 12

Query: Can we see the lovingkindness of God shining upon and inside a person disrespected by our fellows?

OCTOBER 10

Psalm 72:12–14

12 For he shall deliver the needy when he crieth, the poor also, and him that hath no helper.
13 He shall spare the poor and needy, and shall save the souls of the needy.
14 He shall redeem their soul from deceit and violence: and precious shall be their blood in his sight.

Foreigner

There are never any rights for a foreigner, least of all in time of war. No one was required to distinguish the just from the unjust in respect to him.

Fustel de Coulanges (1830–1899)
The Ancient City, (1864; tr. English, 1873),
Garden City, N.Y., Anchor, n.d., p. 206

Query: Query: For whom is our home a sanctuary? Our church? Our nation?

OCTOBER 11

Psalm 16:5–11

5 The LORD is the portion of mine inheritance and of my cup: thou maintainest my lot.
6 The lines are fallen unto me in pleasant places; yea, I have a goodly heritage.
7 I will bless the LORD, who hath given me counsel: my reins also instruct me in the night seasons.
8 I have set the LORD always before me: because he is at my right hand, I shall not be moved.
9 Therefore my heart is glad, and my glory rejoiceth: my flesh also shall rest in hope.
10 For thou wilt not leave my soul in hell: neither wilt thou suffer thine Holy One to see corruption.
11 Thou wilt shew me the path of life: in thy presence is fullness of joy; at thy right hand there are pleasures for evermore.

Conditioning

Wesley had taught the masses to be less concerned with their miserable life on earth, as victims of the Industrial Revolution, than with the life to come; they could now put up with almost anything.

William Sargant,
Battle for the Mind,
New York, Doubleday, 1957, p. 224

Query: Do we control all our choices? Most?

OCTOBER 12

Exodus 33:13–14

13 Now therefore I pray thee, if I have found grace in thy sight, shew me now thy way, that I may know thee, that I may find grace in thy sight: and

consider that this nation is thy people.

14 And he said, My presence shall go with thee, and I will give thee rest.

Hasidim

The core of Hasidic faith was said to consist in their belief that the presence of God permeates and sustains all living matter and in the intense enthusiasm that they impart to their every action. (The Hebrew word 'hasidim' means 'pious ones' – those who are especially dedicated to fulfilling the divinely appointed laws.) The scope of Hasidic devotion extended to all aspects of life, infusing holiness in work, in eating, and in social intercourse.

J.K.Mintz,
Legends of the Hasidim (1968),
University of Chicago, 1974, p. 26

Query: Do we allow the privileges of the scholar, the celebrant, the holy, fully to women? To ourselves?

OCTOBER 13

Psalm 37:24–25

24 Though he fall, he shall not be utterly cast down: for the LORD upholdeth him with his hand.
25 I have been young, and now am old; yet have I not seen the righteous forsaken, nor his seed begging bread.

Beggars and Mini-societies

One of the lasting disgraces of civilization is the rise of the beggars. The few very rich have been balanced by the many poor and, among them, the beggars.

Mini-societies undoubtedly had social failures, but they had no beggars. As group-centered organizations (the only way they could exist) they were egalitarian to an extent unknown among civilized societies. They always shared what they had; so there was no need to beg. If the rugged individualist is on one end of the social teeter-totter, the beggar sits on the other end.

CEWLD

Query: Have we any aid to extend today to one we meet in need or are we, ourselves the ones in need?

OCTOBER 14

Exodus 22:21–23

21 Thou shalt neither vex a stranger, nor oppress him: for ye were strangers in the land of Egypt.
22 Ye shall not afflict any widow or fatherless child.
23 If thou afflict them in any wise and they cry at all unto me, I will surely hear their cry.

Woman as Man's Rib

According to one story in Genesis, God created human beings of both sexes at the same time. According to the second story in Genesis, woman was created out of man's rib. Inasmuch as archaic males knew that all life, male and female, comes out of the female, it would seem that the "rib story" is recognition of male inferiority. To be in first place is to create, and obviously woman creates human life (with of course a little help from the male). The male, to have first place, had to have life coming out of him, particularly woman. So the rib story is a means of assigning primacy to the male—God who creates man and then "out of man" God creates woman.

How otherwise could the ancients justify patriarchy? If the male was to be ruler of life, he also had to be the author or source of life.

CEWLD

Query: Between man and woman, who has power and how is it shared?

OCTOBER 15

Psalm 130:5–5

5 I wait for the LORD, my soul doth wait, and in his word do I hope.

6 My soul waiteth for the LORD more than they that watch for the morning: I say, more than they that watch for the morning.

Women—Courage

When God made people, he made woman from the man's side so that he did not make her from the head or the foot, to be neither man nor woman, but to be like him. Thus the just soul is to be like God, by the side of God, exactly his equal and neither above nor beneath.

Meister Ekhart,
From "Sermon No. 18",
Tr. R.B. Blakney,
Meister Ekhart,
New York, Harper, 1914, p. 180

Query: From whom do we take our life example? Why?

OCTOBER 16

John 15:15

15 Ye have not chosen me, but I have chosen you and ordained you, that ye should go and bring forth much fruit, and that your fruit should remain: that whatsoever ye shall ask of the Father in my name, he may give it to you.

Options

We are all born in a world of options. For some of us, the options are few; for others, the options are many. We rarely know what the options are, when we are young: so if we are active, we often get slapped down. When we are old, we wonder whether life would have been better if we had had precise knowledge of options. For those with fewest options — would they just bow down to 'destiny'? And those with many options — would they have wisdom to choose the most rewarding? And what is finally the 'most rewarding'?

CEWLD

Query: When we speak of a "rewarding life", how is it we judge what the reward is if it is not money?

OCTOBER 17

Psalm 42:8

8 Yet the LORD will command his lovingkindness in the daytime, and in the night his song shall be with me, and my prayer unto the God of my life.

Prophets

The prophets were the creative thinkers of their day, the sources of wisdom. Those who organized religions out of the utterances of the prophets, were the imitative thinkers, the sources of social stasis. The former brought new life to the world; the latter changed the new life into dead forms. The prophet is always in quest of the dynamic, the vibrating, the living, that which is ever bursting into newness, that which glows. The organizer is concerned with order, plant efficiency, the unchanging, and ultimately that which is dead.

CEWLD

Query: Can radical obedience turn into prophetic action? If so, how long before the truth of it is recognized? Does it matter if it takes a generation? Two? More?

OCTOBER 18

Job 13:14–15

14 Wherefore do I take my flesh in my teeth, and put my life in mine hand?
15 Though he slay me, yet will I trust in him: But I will maintain my own ways before him.

Determinism

Man is not 'fully conditioned and determined.' He determines himself whether to give in to conditions or stand up to them. In other words, man is ultimately self-determining. Man does not simply exist, but always decides what his existence will be, what he will become in the next moment.

Victor E. Frankl,
Mankind's Search for Meaning,
New York, Washington Square Press, 1963, p. 206

Query: If I say I will do as I am told, do I give away my power of choice or strengthen that power?

OCTOBER 19

Zechariah 9:12

12 Turn you to the stronghold ye prisoners of hope: even today do I declare that I will render double unto thee:

Straight and Crooked—Portugese Proverb

'Consider the work of God: who can make straight what he has made crooked?'

> *Deus escrive em linkas tortos.*

The Portuguese proverb says literally: 'God writes in lines crooked.' It has been translated: 'God writes straight in crooked lines.'
   The Greek proverb says, literally: 'The dice of God always fall right.' It has been translated: 'The dice of God are always loaded.'

CEWLD

Query: From whom do we accept the interpretation of the word of God? Is it ever proper to exceed the advice of that interpreter?

OCTOBER 20

Psalm 113:9

9 He maketh the barren woman to keep house, and to be a joyful mother of children.

Certainty

Certainty shuts the door on everything but itself. Indeed, it desires to occupy total space and time. Historically, certainty has again and again rejected what is analytically true and what may be holistic truth.

CEWLD

Query: What can be rummaged for the future from an apparent end-of-the-line project, one which is seemingly barren of potentiality? Can we go forward by first going back?

OCTOBER 21

Proverbs 4:23

23 Keep thy heart with all diligence for out of it are the issues of life.

Teaching—(What can be taught)

People must learn to live within bounds. This cannot be taught. Survival depends on people learning fast what they cannot do. They must learn to abstain from unlimited progeny, consumption, and use. It is impossible to educate people for voluntary poverty or to manipulate them into self control. It is impossible to teach joyful renunciation in a world totally structured for higher output and the illusion of declining costs.

Ivan Illich,
Tools for Conviviality,
New York, Harper & Row, 1973, p. 64

Query: How do we know the angels among us? How do we know we are taking the angel's part with another?

OCTOBER 22

Isaiah 19:9–13

9 For this is as the waters of Noah unto me: for as I have sworn that the waters of Noah should no more go over the earth; so have I sworn that I would not be wroth with thee, nor rebuke thee.

10 For the mountains shall depart, and the hills be removed: but my kindness shall not depart from thee, neither shall the covenant of my peace be removed, saith the LORD that hath mercy on thee.

11 O thou afflicted, tossed with tempest and not comforted, behold, I will lay thy stones with fair colours, and lay thy foundations with sapphires.

12 And I will make thy windows of agates, and thy gates of carbuncles, and all thy borders of pleasant stones.

13 And all thy children shall be taught of the LORD; and great shall be the peace of thy children.

Comfort

Greek literature, like the Gospels, '…is a great protest against the modern view that the really important thing is to be comfortable.'

(Quoted material from F.C. Burkitt,
Essays on some Biblical Questions of the Day,
Cambridge, 1909, pp. 208–209)
in: Alfred Zimmern,
The Greek Commonwealth, 5th Ed.,
N.Y. 1961, p. 215

Comfort—2

It is not comfortable to be an inhabitant of this globe.
It never has been, except for brief periods.

Rebecca West,
Black Lands and Grey Falcon, Vol. I
New York, Viking, 1964, p. 50

Query: Will our faith for the day reach from sunup to sundown…and after?

OCTOBER 23

Romans 16:19

19 For your obedience is come abroad unto all men. I am glad therefore in your behalf: but yet I would have you wise unto that which is good and simple concerning evil.

Evil

It is a mistake of considerable consequence to suppose that evil can be neither efficient nor rational; or that rationality is not a neutral capacity to be used for evil as well as good.

Peter Phillips,
The Tragedy of Nazi Germany,
New York, Pegasus, 1970, p. 172

Query: What can be meant by being "wise unto that which is good and simple concerning evil"?

OCTOBER 24

Psalm 104:14–15

14 He causeth the grass to grow for the cattle, and the herb for the service of man: that he may bring forth food out of the earth.
15 And wine that maketh glad the heart of a man, and oil to make his face to shine, and bread which strengtheneth man's heart.

Celibacy

We must keep in mind that celibacy in the most ancient times was a threat to the economy and also a threat to the society. With low life-expectancy, population could be supported solely by compulsory copulation. When populations are low and the life of a society is threatened, celibacy is forbidden. When populations are excessive, birth control becomes the problem. It would be interesting to know when celibacy became a virtue instead of a crime....

CEWLD

Query: Love commitment to God and love commitment to family; are they mutually exclusive for women?

OCTOBER 25

Psalm 25:6

6 Remember, O Lord, thy tender mercies and thy lovingkindnesses;
for they have been ever of old.

Mercy

Agelisaus was questioned upon the justice of this action. 'Inquire only if it
is useful,' said the king; for whenever an action is useful to our country, it
is right.'
This was the international law of ancient cities.

Numa Fustel de Coulanges (1830–1889)
The Ancient City (1864; tr. English 1873)
Garden City, N.Y., Anchor, n.d. p. 206

Query: Is mercy counter-intuitive? Always?

OCTOBER 26

Deuteronomy 1:21

21 Behold, the LORD thy God hath set the land before thee: go up and
possess it, as the LORD God of thy fathers hath said unto thee; fear not,
neither be discouraged.

Faith and Freedom

To the medieval mystic and devout Christian, Meister Eckhart: 'when a
free mind is really disinterested, God is compelled to come into it…. The
soul imbibing God turns into God as the drop becomes the ocean.'

Richard N. Goodwin,
The American Condition (1974),
New York, Bantam, 1975, p. 31

Query: When do we settle for the clarity we have and venture forth into dubious battle? When is our discernment sufficient?

OCTOBER 27

Philippians 1:28

28 And in nothing terrified by your adversaries which is to them an evident token of perdition, but to you salvation, and that of God.

Affirmation

Eckhart was one of the world's great 'Yes-sayers,' whose deep conviction was that untruth or evil is not to be fought with condemnation or criticism, but that it must be displaced by an overwhelming disclosure of the true and the good.

R.B. Blakney,
Meister Eckhart,
New York, Harper & Brothers, 1941,
Introduction, p. xiv

Query: Can we find that of God in our adversaries by affirming them in their heart's desire and by working with them toward achieving it as it aligns with that of God in us?

OCTOBER 28

Isaiah 26:12

12 LORD, thou wilt ordain peace for us for thou also hast wrought all our works in us.

Predestination (Hasidism)

The Baal Shem Tov and his disciples were traveling. While they were riding along the road a leaf floated down and settled upon the lap of the Baal Shem Tov. A bit further on a wind came and blew the leaf from the lap of the Baal Shem Tov to the ground; and there a worm came and crawled onto the leaf and used it for shelter and food. The Baal Shem Tov [Lord Name Good Master of the Good Name] stopped the wagon and called his disciples.

'Look here,' he said. 'When the world was created, even then did the Almighty decree that this leaf should fall on my lap and that a wind should come and take it from my lap and blow it onto the ground where this worm would use it for food and shelter.'

Jerome R. Mintz,
Legends of the Hasidim, (1968),
University of Chicago, 1974, p. 337

Query: How long have we been doing what we are led to do before we hear the Call? Does this equal predestination for those whose mind is stayed on God.

OCTOBER 29

I Corinthians 14:25

25 And thus are the secrets of his heart made manifest; and so falling down upon his face he will worship God, and report that God is in you of a truth.

Marriage

The institution of sacred marriage must be as old in the Indo-European race as the domestic religions; for the one could not exist without the other. This religion taught man that the conjugal union was something more than a relation of the sexes and a fleeting affection, and united man and wife by the powerful bond of the same worship and the same belief. The marriage ceremony too, was so solemn, and produced effects so grave, that it is not surprising that these men did not think it permitted or was possible to have more than one wife in each house. Such a religion could not admit of polygamy.

We can understand, too, that such a marriage was indissoluble, and that divorce was almost impossible....

Fustel de Coulanges (1830–1889),
The Ancient City (1864; tr. Engl. 1873),
Garden City, N.Y., Anchor, n.d. pp. 47–48

CEWLD remark: "Fustel notes that the marriage could be dissolved by a solemn religious rite."

Query: How do the indissoluble bonds between human beings relate to the secrets of the heart and to the will of God? Can we ever guarantee against error?

OCTOBER 30

I Chronicles 28:5–10

5 And of all my sons, (for the LORD hath given me many sons) he hath chosen Solomon for my son to sit upon the throne of the kingdom of the LORD over Israel.
6 And he said unto me, Solomon thy son, he shall build my house and my court for I have chosen him to be my son, and I will be his father.
7 Moreover I will establish his kingdom for ever, if he be constant to do my commandments and my judgments, as at this day.
8 Now therefore in the sight of all Israel the congregation of the LORD and in the audience of our God, keep and seek for all the commandments of the LORD your God: that ye may possess this good land, and leave it for an inheritance for your children after you for ever.
9 And thou, Solomon my son, know thou the God of thy father, and serve him with a perfect heart and with a willing mind; for the LORD searcheth all hearts, and undrstandeth all the imaginations of the thought if thou seek him, he will be found of thee: but if thou forsake him, he will cast thee off for ever.
10 Take heed now: for the LORD hath chosen thee to build an house for the sanctuary: be strong and do it.

Marriage

The question arises, when did marriage become a religious rite? Some contemporary Stone Age societies make little enough of marriage and living in groups as they do, have little or no family sense. The family seemingly cannot come into existence until a man and a woman break out of the group and live by themselves, and the family cannot become a social institution until quite a few households are continued throughout successive generations. This must be a consequence of permanent settlements.

CEWLD

Query: Can we build the house if the LORD is not in and of our plan?

OCTOBER 31

Philippians 1:6

6 Being confident in this very thing, that he which
hath begun a good work in you will perform it....

Order—2

We survive by creating an order out of the chaos of experience. The
order, whether literary,
moral, spiritual, scientific, is fictive. It is created.

CEWLD

Query: What of our work will outlive us?

NOVEMBER

NOVEMBER 1

Acts 27:25

25 Wherefore sirs, be of good cheer: for I believe God that it shall be
even as it was told me.

Identity

1. The organic man is what his genes make him.
2. The social man is what his human surround makes him.
3. The rational man is what his thinking makes him.
4. The spiritual man is what his sense of awe makes him.
5. The whole man is a product of all the external forces and internal
forces that fashion him. The whole man is beyond analysis whether by
himself or by others.

The alien is the human being who has no identity. He is Cain, cut off from all others because of his murderous behavior. The chief figure in the 'Wanderer' laments the loss of all human associations.

Identity, as said earlier in brief form, is a conviction, a certainty, that one belongs, that he has anchorage, *est enim sicut arbor plantata ad rivas aquavium.* (Ps. 1:3), he and 'the other' are forever bound together. He/she belongs (1) to a family (2) a larger group of human beings, (3) to God, (4) to himself, (5) to 'Destiny,' etc. Insofar as a person identifies himself as 'belonging' he cannot suffer alienation. Consider 'belonging to nothingness' to the 'whole.'

CEWLD

Query: How many people does it take to make one's identity group?

NOVEMBER 2

Acts 26:16–19

16 But rise, and stand upon thy feet: for I have appeared unto thee for this purpose, to make thee a minister and a witness both of these things which thou hast seen and of those things to the which I will appear unto thee:
17 Delivering thee from the people, and from the Gentiles, unto whom now I send thee.
18 To open their eyes, and to turn them from darkness to light, and from the power of Satan unto God, that they may receive forgiveness of sins, and inheritance among them which are sanctified by faith that is in me.
19 Whereupon, O king Agrippa, I was not disobedient unto the heavenly vision:

Tsetheck or *Tsedeck*—Rightness, Righteousness

1. What is right, just, normal; rightness, justness of weights and measures a perfect and just weight, *ephah.'*
2. righteousness, in government
3. righteousness, justice, in a case or cause
4. righteousness in speech
5. righteousness, as ethically right
6. righteousness, as justification, vindication

A word like [Hebrew letters] suggests that all subjective value words arise from objective value words. That which is not objective is created by using the objective as a metaphor.

CEWLD

Query: Does the impulse to righteous thought or action come from within or from without one's self?

NOVEMBER 3

Hebrews 10:35–39

35 Cast not away your confidence, which hath great recompense of reward.
36 For ye have need of patience, that, after ye have done the will of God, ye might receive the promise.
37 For yet a little while, and he that shall come will come, and will not tarry.
38 Now the just shall live by faith: but if any man draw back, my soul shall have no pleasure in him.
39 But we are not of them who draw back unto perdition; but of them that believe to the saving of the soul.

Conformance, Conformity

Whoso would be a man must be a nonconformist. He who would gather immortal palms must not be hindered by the name of goodness, but must explore if it be goodness. Nothing is at last sacred but the integrity of your own mind.

Ralph Waldo Emerson,
"Self-Reliance," essay quoted in Geo. C. Clancy,
Thought and its Expression,
New York, Harcourt, Brace, 1928, p. 77

Query: Can we have confidence in a Leading that goes beyond our ability to understand or define it?

NOVEMBER 4

II Corinthians 4:15–18

15 For all things are for your sakes, that the abundant grace might,
through the thanksgiving of many redound to the glory of God.
16 For which cause we faint not; but though our outward man perish, yet
the inward man is renewed day by day.
17 For our light affliction, which is but for a moment, worketh for us a far
more exceeding and eternal weight of glory.
18 While we look not at the things which are seen, but the things which
are not seen: for the things which are seen are temporal, but the things
which are not seen are eternal.

Ten Cardinal Rules

To Rebbe Zusia, he gave the following advice:

Listen, I cannot teach you the ten cardinal rules governing the conduct
of man wishing to serve his Creator. However, there are three things you
can learn from a child and seven you can learn from a thief. From an
infant learn how to laugh, how to cry and how to keep constantly busy.
From the thief? First of all: that whatever he does, he does secretly. Two:
that whatever he does not obtain today, he will try to obtain tomorrow.
Three: he is loyal to his accomplices. Four: he is ready to sacrifice himself
for the object of his desire, even though it may have no value to others.
Five; once the desired object becomes his own, he loses interest. Six: he is
not afraid of hardship. Seven: nothing on earth could make him change
trades, in other words, he does not want to be anyone but himself.

Elie Wiesel,
"The Maggid of Mezeritch," in
Souls on Fire, (1972),
New York, Vintage, 1973, p. 71

Query: To whom does our time primarily belong?

NOVEMBER 5

Matthew 6:2–7

2 Therefore when thou doest thine alms, do not sound a trumpet before

thee, as the hypocrites do in the synagogues and in the streets, that they may have glory of men. Verily I say unto you, They have their reward.
3 But when thou doest alms, let not thy left hand know what thy right hand doeth:
4 That thine alms may be in secret: and thy Father which seeth in secret himself shall reward thee openly.
5 And when thou prayest, thou shalt not be as the hypocrites are: for they love to pray standing in the synagogues and in the streets, that they may be seen of men. Verily I say unto you, They shall have their reward.
6 But thou, when thou prayest, enter into thy closet, and when thou hast shut the door, pray to thy Father which is in secret; and thy Father which seeth in secret shall reward thee openly.
7 But when ye pray, use not vain repetitions as the heathen do; for they think they shall be heard for their much speaking.

Seeing and Doing

1. Often enough we see the danger that we are in, but we may not know what to do, or, knowing, may be reluctant to act.
2. We may see what the problem is, but may not know how to solve it, if indeed there is any solution whatsoever.
3. With hindsight we may see what we should have done but failed to do because of ignorance, greed, ardor, or you-name-it.

CEWLD

Query: What can we learn from hindsight that will give confidence for bold choices in the future and the courage to claim: Yes we CAN!

NOVEMBER 6

John 5:44

44 How can ye believe, which receive honor one of another, and seek not the honor that cometh from God only?

Conformity

Conformity was necessary in tiny societies because they could not afford to quarrel with one another—not even if filled with hate, loathing and a desire to kill. We may also assume that what we call individualism had not revealed itself [in fact, what we call individualism appears to be a product of civilization, a way of thought and behavior, that still has not caught on in much, perhaps most, of the world]. People were almost naturally group-centered, none individual-oriented as a goodly number of Westerners now are. Conformity, given emphasis by tabus was the rule....

CEWLD

Query: If Truth stands alone and you have the truth, what do you do?

NOVEMBER 7

Acts 4:39

39 For the promise is unto you and unto your children and to all that are afar off, even as many as the Lord our God shall call.

Hope

One must eventually arrive in his thinking at a place in which he gives up all hope, all expectations, and at the same time does not register either disappointment or despair. This is what various writers have told us. It is true that the older you get, the more control you have of your responses to experience. Yet can a living person have no hope and be wholly lacking in despair? Is such a one a human being? Sometimes I have a vague feeling as to what these people mean, but I am not sure. In their minds they picture some figure of such control that he is virtually a god. Yet if a god has no compassion, for example, can he show any?

We live on and on... the poets notwithstanding... because positive expectations are greater than negative--otherwise life makes little or no sense.

CEWLD

Query: When hope is repeatedly deferred, how is our prayer affected? When hope is achieved, what then?

NOVEMBER 8

Mark 10:23–27

23 And Jesus looked round about and saith unto his disciples, How hardly shall they that have riches enter into the kingdom of God!
24 And the disciples were astonished at his words. But Jesus answereth again, and saith unto them, Children, How hard is it for them that trust in riches to enter into the kingdom of God!
25 It is easier for a camel to go through the eye of a needle, than for a rich man to enter into the kingdom of God.
26 And they were astonished out of measure, saying among themselves, Who then can be saved?
27 And Jesus looking upon them saith, With man it is impossible, but not with God: for with God all things are possible.

Privacy

To live an entirely private life means above all to be deprived of things essential to a truly human life: to be deprived of the reality that comes from being seen and heard by others, to be deprived of an objective relationship with them that comes from being related to and separated from them through the intermediary of a common world of things, to be deprived of the possibility of achieving something more permanent than life itself. The privation of privacy lies in the absence of others; as far as they are concerned, private man does not appear, and therefore it is as though he did not exist. Whatever he does remains without significance and consequence to others, and what matters to him is without interest to other people.

Hannah Arendt,
The Human Condition (1958),
University of Chicago, 1974, p. 58

Query: Of what significance are our unshared thoughts and discoveries?

NOVEMBER 9

Ecclesiastes 9:17–18

17 The words of wise men are heard in quiet more than
the cry of him that ruleth among fools.
18 Wisdom is better than weapons of war: but one sinner
destroyeth much good.

Foreigner

There are never any rights for a foreigner, least of all in time of war. No one was required to distinguish the just from the unjust in respect to him. Mucius Scaevola and all the Romans believed it was a glorious deed to assassinate an enemy. The consul Marcius boasted publicly of having deceived the king of Macedonia. Paulus Aemilius sold as slaves a hundred thousand Epirots who had voluntarily surrendered themselves to him.

The Lacedaemonian Phebidas seized upon the citadel of the Thebans in time of peace. Agesilaus was questioned upon the justice of this action. 'Inquire only if it is useful,' said the king; 'for whenever an action is useful to our country, it is right.' This was the international law of ancient cities. Another king of Sparta, Cleomenes, said that all the evil one could do to enemies was always just in the eyes of gods and man.

The conqueror could use his victory as he pleased. No human or divine law restrained his vengeance or his cupidity.

These men made war not only upon soldiers, but upon an entire population, men, women, children, and slaves. They waged it not only against human beings, but against fields and crops. They burned down houses and cut down trees.

Numa Fustel de Coulanges (1830–1889)
The Ancient City (1864; tr. English 1873)
Garden City, N.Y., Anchor, n.d., pp. 206–207

Query: When is it wrong to speak truth to power? When is it right?

NOVEMBER 10

I Timothy 4:1–3

1 Now the Spirit speaketh expressly, that in the latter times some shall depart from the faith giving heed to seducing spirits and doctrines of devils;
2 Speaking lies in hypocrisy; having their conscience seared with a hot iron;
3 Forbidding to marry, and commanding to abstain from meats, which God hath created to be received with thanksgiving of them which believe and know the truth.

Taboo

The ideas of taboo became transformed into ideas of purity and impurity when they were associated with a belief in the gods. Above all else, the gods demand purity in those who approach them.

Martin P. Nilsson,
A History of Greek Religion, (1975), Second Edition, Revised, (1952)
New York, Norton, 1964, p. 82

Query: How does the Holy hear the pleas of those not yet restored or redeemed?

NOVEMBER 11

James 2:14–16

14 What doth it profit, my brethren, though a man say he hath faith, and hath not works? Can faith save him?
15 If a brother or sister be naked and destitute of daily food,
16 And one of you says unto them, Depart in peace, be ye warmed and filled; notwithstanding ye give them not those things which are needful to the body; what doth it profit?
17 Even so, faith, if it hath not works, is dead, being alone.

Hungry, The

It is all very well, after a night's untroubled sleep, followed by a delicious breakfast, to preach to hungry people that they are not to set their minds on earthly comforts. First feed the hungry, as Jesus did, before you begin to preach.

Rudolf F. Kurtz
Journal of RFK,
University of Nebraska, 1970, p. 153

Query: In the questing and seeking this day, what is our first priority and how is energy to put behind the quest accessed?

NOVEMBER 12

Psalm 37:3–7

3 Trust in the LORD, and do good; so shalt thou dwell in the land, and verily thou shalt be fed.
4 Delight thyself also in the LORD; and he shall give thee the desires of thine heart.
5 Commit thy way unto the LORD; trust also in him; and he shall bring it to pass.
6 And he shall bring forth thy righteousness as the light, and thy judgment as the noonday.

Hunger and Thirst

Blessed are those who hunger and thirst for righteousness....
You can say it in a thousand languages and the effect will be the same. It sounds fine in church. You can feel pious as you mouth the words.
In the academic world we can also hunger and thirst for understanding, for knowledge, for wisdom, and the world of academia can talk of wisdom as though it were a sacrament....

CEWLD

Query: We are promised if we hunger and thirst after righteousness we will be filled. How will we know we are filled? Will the hunger and thirst end?

NOVEMBER 13

Hebrews 13:18

18 Pray for us for we trust we have a good conscience, in all things willing to live honestly.

Honest People

It is quite possible, as a lawyer once declared emphatically. 'There are lots of honest people around!' Yet we can never be sure of people until they are tested in situations which invite dishonesty as well as honesty. Honesty too often is the absence of temptation to be dishonest (coupled with an excellent chance not to be discovered —better yet, not to be suspected). History tells us over and over again that power corrupts, and some scholars have gone so far as to state that power always corrupts! It is so pleasant to think of the majority of us as fine, upstanding members of the 'human race.' Charles Peguey thought only a handful of people were really honest. When one looks in the mirror, the tendency is to agree with Peguey. Yet since we like comparing, we state that like sheep we have all gone astray. And we are greatly comforted to read the words attributed to Jesus, making it clear that God alone is good.

CEWLD

Query: Is there a point in our past when we were most tempted to sell out? Why did we choose as we did?

NOVEMBER 14

II Peter 1:19

19 We have also a more sure word of prophecy; whereunto ye do well that ye take heed, as unto a light that shineth in a dark place until the day dawn, and the day star arise in your heart

Darkness and Light

In the second verse of Genesis we are told that darkness was everywhere. The fiery first act of creation is the creation of light. The darkness no longer rules absolutely: it is now contained in the night. Now, to be sure, if different phases of creation were to occur on different days, light had to be created at the very beginning. What Elohim created had to be visible, had to be seen.

In the *Gospel According to John*, the first chapter treats the light and darkness symbolically. It is now the darkness of the mind and the spirit that has to be dispelled by the light of understanding. 'The true light that enlightens every man was coming into the world.' Jesus, representing spiritual illumination, has come into the world to dispel the darkness of ignorance, untruth, and sin.

CEWLD

Query: We say "Things will look different in the morning" and then hardly pause to wonder why they do. Why wasn't the perspective of the dawn available at the midnight hour?

NOVEMBER 15

Hebrews 6:9

9 But beloved, we are persuaded better things of you, and things that accompany salvation, though we thus speak.
10 For God is not unrighteous to forget your work and labour of love, which ye have shewed toward his name, in that ye have ministered to the saints, and do minister.
11 And we desire that every one of you do shew the same diligence to the full assurance of hope unto the end:
12 That ye be not slothful, but followers of them who through faith and patience inherit the promises.

Forgiveness

"Seventy times seven"— Matthew 18:22 [We must not forget that the number seven was of extraordinary significance.] Note that in Matthew 18:15–35, forgiveness is commanded. This raises questions about commandments to love, to forgive, to be good. We can command people not to hurt one another and exact laws to cover many of the hurts. It is not possible, however, to compel people to love, to forgive, to be sensitive, to respect their fellow human beings.

CEWLD

Query: Can we genuinely feel as we are commanded to feel? What happens when we cannot attain the mark and fail to find peace with the failure?

NOVEMBER 16

Joel 3:14

14 Multitudes, multitudes in the valley of decision: for the day of the LORD is near in the valley of decision.

Decisions

Insofar as we ask other people to make decisions regarding what we should do and say, we are not mature. Nor can we be moral or immoral. A robot, well programmed, may make excellent decisions in the area for which it has been adjusted, but these are not the robot's own decisions. A computing machine is not a human being but a human product.

To decide personally is to assume personal responsibility. To parrot someone else is to take up responsibility for that other person's decisions. In other words, to use the decisions of others is to be either a beneficiary or a victim of someone else's solution to a given problem.

CEWLD

Query: How do we prioritize risks and goals against principles —with integrity?

NOVEMBER 17

Jeremiah 8:20–22

20 The harvest is past, the summer is ended, and we are not saved.
21 For the hurt of the daughter of my people am I hurt; I am black; astonishment hath taken hold on me.
22 Is there no balm in Gilead; is there no physician there? Why then is not the health of the daughter of my people recovered?

Danger in Lucidity

Though outwardly rough, Moshe possesses a disarming kindness. In exchange for a single word, a single smile, he would give you his only shirt, his share of happiness. Let a beggar fall sick, he'll go begging in his place. He becomes dangerous only in his fits of lucidity. Whenever he feels them coming on, he asks to be locked up.

Elie Wiesel,
A Beggar in Jerusalem, (1970)
New York, Avon, 1971, p. 41

Query: Trusting to dreams, visions, callings or leadings, do we do so independent of advice?

NOVEMBER 18

Psalm 4:4

4 Stand in awe, and sin not: commune with your own heart upon your bed, and be still. Selah.

Women

In a patriarchal society, woman had significance only if (1) she was the daughter of a significant man, (2) the wife of a significant man, (3) the mother of a significant man, (4) was a queen, (5) became an outstanding criminal.

CEWLD

Query: Is one human being responsible only for his/her fate or can the responsibility for the fate of another be assumed, even if just for a time? Consider motherhood and the bonds of family as examples.

NOVEMBER 19

Job 23:13–14

13 But he is in one mind, and who can turn him? And what his soul desireth, even that he doeth.
14 For he performeth the thing that is appointed for me: and many such things are with him.

Power

Power has never been adequately defined. It is in fact a quality like combustibility, for it depends on the spark of an individual personality to ignite it successfully....

Eugene Kennedy
"Political Power and American Ambivalence"
The New York Times Magazine, March 19, 1978, p. 19

Query: Can we know our power outside the exercising of it? God's power in us, the same?

NOVEMBER 20

Luke 13:24

24 Strive to enter in at the strait gate: for many, I say unto you, will seek to enter in, and will not be able.

Power—2

No matter how it is acquired…it is exercised only by the decision and act of an individual.

Eugene Kennedy
"Political Power and American Ambivalence,"
The New York Times Magazine, March 18, 1978, p. 19

Query: Can one have power without authority?

NOVEMBER 21

Deuteronomy 6:32

32 Ye shall observe to do therefore as the LORD your God commanded you, that ye may live, and that it may be well with you, and that ye may prolong your days in the land which ye shall possess.

Immortality

The fact…that immortality cannot be 'proved' is not very important, for nothing of any importance can be 'proved' anyway. All life is a matter of faith, and the task of the honest man is to find a reasonable faith.

David Elton Trueblood,
From the Foreword to *Spirit in Man*,
Rufus Matthew Jones (1863–1948),
Stanford University, 1941, pp. viii–ix

Query: Can or do we claim the "promise" of the "commandments with promise"?

NOVEMBER 22

John 9:4

4 I must work the works of him that sent me, while it is day: the night cometh, when no man can work.

Present, The

It is only occasionally when I think of day and night, the passing of the seasons, the changes in my physical (biological) form and my body capacities that I become conscious of time as motion. For the most part I have lived and continue to live in what I call "the continuous present."

CEWLD

Query: For the Now, how may we become more fully present to the moment?

NOVEMBER 23

Psalm 37:23

23 The steps of a good man are ordered by the LORD and he delighteth in his way.

Order

We cultivate order for the sake of economic efficiency; we insist on individualism (disorder) for the sake of our humanity.

CEWLD

Query: When we go against established order, what is our authority?

NOVEMBER 24

Luke 11:36

36 If thy whole body therefore be full of light, having no part dark, the whole shall be full of light, as when the bright shining of a candle does give thee light.

The 'I'

'I' am the only one who may not give voice to his sufferings. In fact, 'I' am not allowed to suffer, for 'I' must be the vessel into which the plaints of the world are poured. It is a difficult role to play, for 'I' am just one of the innumerable organisms of this world, only one of 4 billion human beings on this earth, only one among so many adults, only one among so many adult males, only one among so many male septuagenarians (almost 'octo-'). 'I' sometimes feel like reciting some of the lines of Shakespeare's Shylock. Strange as it may seem, even 'I' bleed when my flesh is cut.

CEWLD

Query: What do we do when another sees our Light and we do not feel filled with it?

NOVEMBER 25

Romans 15:4

4 For whatsoever things were written aforetime were written for our learning that we through patience and comfort of the scriptures might have hope.

Private and Public

The privation of privacy lies in the absence of others; as far as they are concerned, private man does not appear, and therefore it is as though he did not exist. Whatever he does remains without significance and consequence to others, and what matters to him is without interest to other people.

Hannah Arendt,
The Human Condition (1958),

University of Chicago, 1974, p. 58

Query: What impels us to bring our private leadings into a public forum?

NOVEMBER 26

Proverbs 23:23

23 Buy the truth and sell it not: also wisdom, and instruction, and understanding.

God

Such as men themselves are, such will God Himself seem to them to be.

John Smith,
The Platonist,
Cited by Aldous Huxley,
The Perennial Philosophy,
Harper, 1970, p. 144

Query: Is there an individual to whom grace is not extended? Do we ever feel excluded from the reach of grace? Are we?

NOVEMBER 27

Proverbs 22:1–2

1 A good name is rather to be chosen than great riches, and loving favour rather than silver and gold.
2 The rich and poor meet together: the LORD is the maker of them all.

Das Ding an Sich [The Thing in Itself]

Percy Bridgman wrote a book which was given the title: "The Way Things Are."
We may say that things are the way they are because we are the way we are. Were we other than what we are our perspective would be other than what it is. It follows that human beings can never initially grasp anything in its ultimate essence or being or state of form or whatever reveals *das Ding an sich.*

CEWLD

Query: What factors lead us to trust in the insights of another today? In scripture? In our own leadings?

NOVEMBER 28

Hebrews 13:17

17 Obey them that have the rule over you, and submit yourselves for they watch for your souls, as they that must give account, that they may do it with joy, and not with grief: for that is unprofitable for you.

Difference

...a philosopher who gains a following is deemed, at least temporarily, superior to one who is ignored; so too the scientist, the scholar. Things may in the future change, but there are always contemporary judgments of one kind or another stressing superiority and implying inferiority.

CEWLD

Query: Who influences the hidden authorities and from whence does their power derive?

NOVEMBER 29

Proverbs 24:5–6

5 A wise man is strong: yea, a man of knowledge increaseth strength.
6 For by wise counsel thou shalt make thy war: and in multitude of counselors there is safety.

Biography of a God

The biography of a god can be written only as a phase of the life process of a people.

A.Eustace Haydon,
Biography of the Gods,
New York, Macmillan, 1941, p. 16

Query: Is God limited by the bounds of our comprehension?

NOVEMBER 30

Timothy 1:8

8 But we know that the law is good, if a man use it lawfully;

God

Had I a God, whom I could understand, I would no longer hold him for God.

Meister Eckhart,
Cited by Rudolf Otto,
Mysticism East and West,
New York, Macmillan, 1970, p. 42

Query: When led by the Spirit, what are our options other than to do? To demur? To wait? Then what happens?

☙DECEMBER☙

DECEMBER 1

Psalm 37:3–6

3 Trust in the LORD, and do good; so shalt thou be fed.
4 Delight thyself also in the LORD; and he shall give thee the desires of thine heart.
5 Commit thy way unto the LORD; trust also in him; and he shall bring it to pass.

6 And he shall bring forth thy righteousness as the light, and thy judgment as the noonday.

Justice:

Justice does not rest on affection, or there would be very little of it.
Richard N. Goodwin,
The American Condition, (1974),
New York, Bantam, 1975, p. 107

Query: Do we recognize justice when it has been done? Do we recognize it right away?

DECEMBER 2

Exodus 24:7

7 And he took the book of the covenant and read in the audience of the people: and they said, All that the LORD hath said will we do, and be obedient.

Social Classes

In a nomad civilization there are simply families. They may be rich or poor, but the tribe is not divided into different social classes. Some tribes are 'nobler' than others, but all Bedouin regard themselves as 'noble' compared with the settled cultivators. Even slaves do not constitute a class apart: they form part of the family.

Roland de Vaux,
Ancient Israel,
New York, McGraw-Hill, 1965, p. 68

Query: Whom do we obey without question?

DECEMBER 3

Proverbs 22:2

2 The rich and the poor meet together: The LORD is the maker of them all.

Business Exchange

And so, giving or taking here, in order to recover or pay out there, that is properly called 'exchange.' And this practice was invented principally for the convenience of trade….

Ludovico Guicciardini,
"Antwerp, the Great Market,"
In *The Description of the Low Countries Gathered into an Epitome (English Experience, No 804),*
Walter J. Johnson, 1977, p. 198

Query: In a business exchange, whose advantage is primary? For what period of time?

DECEMBER 4

Isaiah 32:8

8 But the liberal deviseth liberal things and by liberal things shall he stand.

Young-Old

The young are working on the early chapters. The old are busy designing personal colophons.

CEWLD

Query: In the inheritance exchanges, do we recognize what we receive? What we bequeath?

DECEMBER 5

Ezekiel 16:8

8 Now when I passed by thee, and looked upon thee, behold, thy time was the time of love; and I spread my skirt over thee, and covered thy nakedness yea, I sware unto thee and entered into a covenant with thee, saith the Lord God, and thou becamest mine.

Historian

The historian, like other specialists, easily imagines that his own pocket of thinking is the whole universe of thought, and easily assumes a sovereign finality or ascendancy for his own branch of study.

Herbert Butterfield,
Man on his Past,
Cambridge Univ. Press, 1953, 1969, p. 18

Query: Can we fully enter into the observation point of another person who is a participant in our own personal drama?

DECEMBER 6

Isaiah 11:10

10 And in that day there shall be a root of Jesse, which shall stand for an ensign of the people; to it shall the Gentiles seek; and his rest shall be glorious.

Wisdom

The wise know that the individual is not and cannot be free and therefore, in expressing the will of God…they become free. He who would gain his life must lose it…."

W.I.Thompson,
At the Edge of History,
New York, Harper, 1971, p. 120

Query: Can the wise understand the past, weigh the present and prepare for the future…or how much should they or we labor to do so?

DECEMBER 7

Jeremiah 33:15

15 In those days, and at that time, will I cause the Branch of righteousness

to grow up unto David; and he shall execute judgment and righteousness in the land.

God

In any comprehensive view of the great and small mythological systems out of which the beliefs of mankind have been drawn, the biblical idea of God must be clearly set apart, as representing a principle nowhere else exclusively affirmed; namely, of the absolute transcendence of divinity.

Joseph Campbell,
The Masks of God: Occidental Mythology,
New York, Viking, 1971, pp. 108–109

Query: The History that flows through us today, can we bless and release it into the Future?

DECEMBER 8

Romans 4:5–8

5 But to him that worketh not, but believeth on him that justifieth the ungodly, his faith is counted for righteousness.
6 Even as David also describeth the blessedness of the man, unto whom God imputeth righteousness without works,
7 Saying, Blessed are they whose iniquities are forgiven and whose sins are covered.
8 Blessed is the man to whom the Lord will not impute sin.

Difference: Superior and Inferior

It is true that we have … superiority and inferiority in human capacities. A superior voice in hog-calling is one that presumably brings in the hogs; a superior voice in operatic singing is one that most successfully recreates what is in the musical score. Both hog-calling and operatic singing require voices, but superiority and inferiority exist with the small class of each and not between the classes.

Archaeological museums testify to what has survived and been catalogued and housed of objective remains of earlier times; art galleries, however, stress excellence as well as mere survival.

Again a philosopher who gains a following is deemed, at least temporarily, superior to one who is ignored; so too, the scientist, the scholar. Things may in the future change, but there are always contemporary judgments of one kind or another stressing superiority and implying inferiority.

CEWLD

Query: How wide is our ability to extend Grace to each other? How deep is our ability to accept Grace for ourselves?

DECEMBER 9

Psalm 18:25–29

25 With the merciful thou wilt shew thyself merciful; with an upright man thou wilt shew thyself upright;
26 With the pure thou wilt shew thyself pure; and with the forward thou wilt shew thyself forward.
27 For thou wild save the afflicted people; but wilt bring down high looks.
28 For thou wilt light my candle: the LORD my God will enlighten my darkness.
29 For by thee I have run through a troop; and by my God have I leaped over a wall.

Historian

The historian, like other specialists, easily imagines that his own pocket of thinking is the whole universe of thought, and easily assumes a sovereign finality or ascendancy for his own branch of study.

Herbert Butterfield,
Man on his Past,
Cambridge University Press, 1969, p. 18

Query: The lighting of a candle, the removal of a shoe, do we see the changes coming?

DECEMBER 10

I Timothy 1:4–5

4 Neither give heed to fables and endless genealogies, which minister
questions, rather than godly edifying which is in faith: so do.
5 Now the end of the commandment is charity out of a pure heart, and
of a good conscience and of faith unfeigned:

Reverence

The years from 1914 to 1932 were a time of questioning. The thrust
of the period was toward a single standard society which broke down
the old cleavages of sex and social status. Intellectuals led the assault
on the groups which had traditionally exercised moral authority, but the
'revolution in morals' would have taken place without them. The nation
had lost its fear of the wrath of God and its faith in the nineteenth
century moral standards the churches had supported. It no longer had
the same reverence for the old mores, and it was determined to free itself
from the harsh imperatives of religious asceticism.

William E. Leuchtenburg,
The Perils of Prosperity, 1914–1932, (1958),
Chicago, University of Chicago, 1973, p. 7

DECEMBER 11

Psalm 34:8

8 O taste and see that the LORD is good: blessed is the man that trusted
in him.

Family

The members of the ancient family were united by something more
powerful than birth, affection, or physical strength; this was the religion
of the sacred fire, and of dead ancestors. The ancient family was a religion
rather than a natural association. Religion, it is true, did not create the
family, but certainly it gave the family its rules; and hence it comes that
the constitution of the ancient family was so different from what it would
have been if it had owed its foundation to natural affection.

Numa Denis Fustel de Coulanges (1830–1889),
The Ancient City (1864; trans. Eng., 1873),

Garden City, N.Y., Anchor, n.d., p. 42

Query: The Key to the City, the Stranger at the Gate, how tied are we to place and community?

DECEMBER 12

Joel 2:25

25 And I will restore to you the years that the locust hath eaten.

Family

The belief relative to the dead, and to the worship that was due them, founded the ancient family, and gave it the greater part of its rules.

Numa Denis Fustel de Coulanges (1830–1889),
The Ancient City (1864; trans. Eng., 1873),
Garden City, N.Y., Anchor, n.d., p. 48

Query: Kinship, how does it relate to eternity?

DECEMBER 13

Philemon Ver. 25

25 The grace of our Lord Jesus Christ be with your spirit. Amen.

Spirit, Power of

The religious organizations have no faith in the power of the spirit. They believe in Material Power by means of which one no longer has to urge— one can dictate!

Material authority thus is accepted as greater than spiritual power.

CEWLD

Query: Does one leave a spiritual legacy?

DECEMBER 14

Proverbs 16:32

32 He that is slow to anger is better than the mighty and he that ruleth his spirit than he that taketh a city.

Rule

'What,' he [Confucius] asked, 'has one who is not able to govern himself to do with governing others.'

Elias Canetti,
Crowds and Power,
New York, Compass, 1966, p. 210

Query: If someone is waiting for our wisdom or advice and comes upon us suddenly for it, what is our inner response?

DECEMBER 15

Hebrews 10:35–39

35 Cast not away therefore your confidence, which hath great recompence of reward.
36 For ye have need of patience, that, after ye have done the will of God, ye might receive the promise.
37 For yet a little while, and he that shall come will come, and will not tarry.
38 Now the just shall live by faith: but if any man draw back, my soul shall have no pleasure in him.
39 But we are not of them who draw back unto perdition; but of them who believe unto the saving of the soul.

Anyone who takes the sure road is as good as dead.

C.G. Jung,
Memories, Dreams, Reflections,
New York, Vintage, 1963, p. 246.

Query: Can we go forward without certainty? Alone? Leading others?

DECEMBER 16

II Samuel 23:5

5 Although my house be not so with God; yet he hath made with me an everlasting covenant, ordered in all things, and sure: for this is all my salvation, and all my desire, although he maketh it not to grow.

Suffer

People who think deeply and those who respond to all situations instinctively, people who are creative and those who are lacking in all skills have one thing in common: they all suffer. Sometimes I think that only a creature like Hasek's Schweik [*The Good Soldier Svejk: and His Fortunes in the World War*, Jaroslav Hasek, Penguin] escapes suffering. And Schweik, we remember, is a fictional creature.

CEWLD

Query: King David looked on his legacy and his house at his deathbed and thanked God rather for his relationship than for his progeny. Which is our main source of gratitude? Does our relationship die with us?

DECEMBER 17

Job 42:15–17

15 And in all the land were no women found so fair as the daughters of Job: and their father gave them inheritance among their brethren.
16 After this lived Job an hundred and forty years, and saw his sons, and his sons' sons, even four generations.
17 So Job died, being old and full of days.

The Center

The true world is always in the middle, at the Center....

Mircea Eliade,

The Sacred and the Profane,
New York, Harcourt, Brace, & World, 1954, p. 42

Query: How much can we pass on to our family of what we live out from our Center? Can we interpret our Inner Voice so they will understand and make sense of our lived-out lives?

DECEMBER 18

Matthew 1:1–6, 16–17

1 The book of the generations of Jesus Christ, the son of David, the son of Abraham.
2 Abraham begat Isaac and Isaac begat Jacob; and Jacob begat Judas and his brethren;
3 And Judas begat Phares and Zara of Thamar; and Phares begat Esrom and Esrom begat Aram;
4 And Aram begat Aminadab; and Aminadab begat Naason; and Naason begat Salmon;
5 And Salmon begat Booz of Rachab; and Booz begat Obed of Ruth; and Obed begat Jesse;
6 And Jesse begat David the king;
16 And Jacob begat Joseph the husband of Mary, of whom was born Jesus, who is called Christ.
17 So all the generations from Abraham to David are fourteen generations and from David until the carrying away into Babylon are fourteen generations and from the carrying away into Babylon unto Christ are fourteen generations.

Certainty

We must hold clearly in mind that there is no possible way for us to attain certainty concerning things which pass our understanding.

C.G. Jung,
Memories, Dreams, Reflections,
New York, Vintage, 1963, p. 300

Query: Should we know of a certainty a bold decision would affect and change the generations of our family forever, would our boldness be diminished or increased?

DECEMBER 19

Proverbs 4:3

3 For I was my father's son, tender and only beloved in the sight of my mother.
Certainty—2

There is nothing I am quite sure about. I have no definite convictions— not about anything. I know only that I was born and exist, and it seems to me that I have been carried along. I exit on the foundation of something I do not know. In spite of all uncertainties, I feel a solidity underlying all existence and a continuity in my mode of being.

The world into which we are born is brutal and cruel, and at the same time of divine beauty.

C.G.Jung,
Memories, Dreams, Reflections,
New York, Vintage, 1963, p. 358

Query: Do we trust in the love and benevolence of another? Of others? Of family? When we are old?

DECEMBER 20

Psalm 113:9

9 He maketh the barren woman to keep house, and to be a joyful mother of children.

Certainty—3

Certainty shuts the door on everything but itself. Indeed, it desires to occupy total space and time. Historically, certainty has again and again rejected what is analytically true and what may be holistic truth.

CEWLD

Query: What can be rummaged for the future from an apparent end-of-the-line project, one which is seemingly barren of potentiality? Can we go forward by first going back?

DECEMBER 21

Psalm 126:1–6

1 When the LORD turned again the captivity of Zion, we were like them that dream.
2 Then was our mouth filled with laughter, and our tongue with singing: then said they among the heathen, the LORD hath done great things for them.
3 The LORD hath done great things for us; whereof we are glad.
4 Turn again our captivity, O LORD, as the stream in the south.
5 They that sow in tears shall reap in joy.
6 He that goeth forth and weepeth, bearing precious seed, shall doubtless come again with rejoicing, bringing his sheaves with him.

Present, The

For all human beings, it is always NOW. Unless one deliberately stops to think about it, life is not a succession of points of time; it is continuous. Even when I watch the second hand of a watch, I can think of a specious present only by forcing myself to do so.... I am not hurrying along from moment to moment. Even as I walk or run or move about in the day's work ...I remain I—Me—no matter what happens around me....

CEWLD

Query: In the present moment, what are we carrying as baggage?

DECEMBER 22

Psalm 71:17–21

17 O God, thou hast taught me from my youth: and hitherto have I declared thy wondrous works.
18 Now also when I am old and greyheaded, O God, forsake me not: until I have shewed thy strength unto this generation, and thy power to

every one that is to come.

19 Thy righteousness also, O God, is very high, who hast done great thing O God, who is like unto thee!

20 Thou, which hast shewed me great and sore troubles, shalt quicken me again, and shalt bring me up again from the depths of the earth.

21 Thou shalt increase my greatness and comfort me on every side.

Certainty

There is, for example, no certainty about the measuring devices since they were arbitrarily set up. Obviously what we produce is something a bit laughable: "a relative certainty." We may reasonably wonder if all our certainties are oxymoronic!

CEWLD

Query: Are the certainties we hold in age the same as those we hold in youth? Do they increase or decrease in number and strength?

DECEMBER 23

Job 11:17

17 And thine age shall be clearer than the noonday; thou shalt shine forth, thou shalt be as the morning.

Certainty

What ... man wants is a sense of certainty in a world that seems uncertain. He wants a sense of meaning where meaning seems lost. He wants hope in a miasma of bleak hopelessness....

Peter Phillips,
The Tragedy of Nazi Germany,
Pegasus, 1970, p. 83

Query: What do we do with our certainty? How long does it last?

DECEMBER 24

Luke 2:4–7

4 And Joseph went up from Galilee, out of the city of Nazareth, into Judea, unto the city of David, which is called Bethlehem; (because he was of the house and lineage of David):)
5 To be taxed with Mary his espoused wife, being great with child.
6 And so it was, that, while they were there, the days were accomplished that she should be delivered.
7 And she brought forth her firstborn son, and wrapped him in swaddling clothes, and laid him in a manger; because there was no room for them in the inn.

Calling

The artist, the scientist, the thinker—all have to keep doggedly at their creative work, even when no one is interested in them or their work or has any confidence in either. [Likewise do we, called in our uniqueness to the designed-for-us Calling of God. Ed.]

CEWLD

Query: If we are shunned or excluded from the community we are called to serve, how do we live and move and have our being in it in obedience to our Calling?

DECEMBER 25

Jeremiah 23:23–24

23 Am I a God at hand, saith the LORD, and not a God afar off?
24 Can any hide himself in secret places that I shall not see him? saith the LORD. Do I not fill heaven and earth? saith the LORD.

Biography

Biography is always a work of the imagination.

R.R. Glover,
The Conflict of Religions in the Early Roman Empire,
Boston, Beacon, 1960, p. 116

Query: What truths of another (or of ourselves) do we record in memoir or journal writing? By what standard—of objective or subjective reasoning—do we choose our observations of their personal truths?

DECEMBER 26

Proverbs 23:23

23 Buy the truth and sell it not: also wisdom, and instruction, and understanding.

God

Such as men themselves are, such will God Himself seem to them to be.

John Smith,
The Platonist,
Cited by Aldous Huxley,
The Perennial Philosophy,
New York, Harper, 1970, p. 144

Query: Can we "permit" God to exceed our own ability to understand God? How and when do we learn to do so?

DECEMBER 27

Jeremiah 33:11

11 The voice of joy, and the voice of gladness, the voice of the bride-groom, and the voice of the bride, the voice of them that shall say, Praise the LORD of host for the LORD is good; for his mercy endureth for ever: and of them that shall bring the sacrifice of praise into the house of the LORD. For I will cause to return the captivity of the land, as at the first saith the LORD.

Biography—2

The ancients did not feel—nor perhaps did the moderns before Rousseau wrote his Confessions—that there could be any permanent or public interest in the minutiae of personal life. A man's work, or his large acts on the world's stage, were all they thought worth remembering; and, if they wanted more, they were apt to invent a myth which would satisfy their fancy or their sense of fitness, like the story of Herodotus reading his History at the Olympic Games and of the boy Thucydides, as he listened, bursting into tears of admiration.

Aubrey de Selincourt,
The World of Herodotus,
Boston, Little, Brown, & Co., 1962, p. 33

(CEWLD comment: In group-centered societies, human figures tend to become types—even the "rugged individualist" stands for a class of people rather than particular persons. In the societies that are individual-oriented, the types tend to give way to emerging individuals. Types are very much alike and know it; individuals are unique and may therefore be curious about the details of other individuals' lives. This needs study: Biography in group-centered societies and individual-oriented societies.)

Query: If we live or die we are the LORD's (Romans 14:8). So how much do others need to know?

DECEMBER 28

Acts 24:14–16

[Paul before Felix in Rome]

14 But this I confess unto thee, that after the way which they call heresy, so worship I the God of my fathers, believing all things which are written in the law and in the prophets,
15 And have hope toward God, which they themselves also allow, that there shall be a resurrection of the dead, both of the just and unjust.

Biography—3

When a person dies, how much of him disappears forever cannot always (if ever) be known. Some people seem to live very simple lives; yet at times they startle us with utterances revealing a train of thought never before suspected. Other people are much involved in the world of their times, are in the public almost constantly, write a good deal, and talk a great deal more. When they die, how much remains unspoken, unwritten, very definitely in consciousness but unreleased? What of ourselves to we keep to ourselves and for ourselves to death itself? Is H.H. H. [Sen. Hubert Horatio Humphrey] as garrulous and outgoing as he seems [1971]? On the other hand are there really any inscrutable men or women or are we all finally scrutable?

Inasmuch as the totality of a given man or woman is never observed completely and disinterestedly and never recorded, death carries away into oblivion that which can never be recovered. Much of that which is lost is well lost; a little, perhaps, would have been invaluable.

CEWLD

Query: Those who keep silent on the secrets of others, are they then dull conversationalists? Do we put the confidences placed in us permanently away from any view or writing?

DECEMBER 29

Psalm 138:3

3 In the day when I cried thou answeredst me, and strengthenedst me with strength in my soul.

Strength and Weakness

We talk about our 'real' friends in terms of their strength; our enemies in terms of their weakness. After all who can note the faults of a beloved friend, or find the merit in a despicable enemy?

As I have so often been reminded—we mustn't expect too much of ourselves. Again and again, I call to mind the utterance of 'a good Christian' woman: 'God doesn't expect too much of us.'

Perhaps like this woman's God, we should lower our expectations!

CEWLD

Query: If we do note the faults in a beloved friend or the merits in a declared enemy, what then?

DECEMBER 30

Luke 10:29

29 But he, willing to justify himself, said unto Jesus, And who is my neighbor?

Neighbors

It is women rather than men who have neighbors.

CEWLD

Query: How far into our lives, into our hearts, do we let enter the one(s) who love us?

DECEMBER 31

Psalm 102:16–21

16 When the LORD shall build up Zion, he shall appear in all his glory:
17 He will regard the prayer of the destitute, and not despise their prayer.
18 This shall be written for the generation to come: and the people which shall be created shall praise the LORD.

Obituary

Are nice things said about the dead because our predecessors were afraid of their ghosts? Since in the past only the people of the ruling classes had obituaries, were the nice things said because princes and other noblemen were thought to continue ruling from the grave?

Nowadays of course in our obituaries we try to give the dead the 'breaks,' chiefly on behalf of the survivors. Yet we are probably doing something very ancient—telling the dead soothingly, 'O You Nice Person You! You are so wonderful, wise, and benevolent that you will only be good to those you left here. You won't haunt us or do strange things at night will you? Don't frighten us. We'll bring offerings to your shrine and [this is not said aloud but we'll include it] ' —for all that we do for you please reward us tenfold, a hundredfold, a thousandfold—all the folding stuff you can lay hold on!')

CEWLD

Query: If our good deeds are done anonymously in life, do we leave a record of them as obituary or do we leave them to travel the human connection unrecorded? What of all the unwritten miracles of Jesus and of the disciples and believers whose names are mentioned once or even ignored in the Bible? At significant points, a person, with no name given, was the hinge on which history turned. Is Anonymous enough?

Quaker Abbey Press, LLC

Quaker Abbey Press, LLC

Located in Portland, Oregon at 4819 SE 70th Ave, zip code 97206, Quaker Abbey Press has been in operation since 2007. See facebook pages for Rosalie V. Grafe and for Quaker Abbey for works in progress and daily postings. Order books postage paid at the webpage: quakerabbeypress.com or mail a check to Rosalie Grafe at the above address.

See quakerabbeypress.com in 2011 for our titles as they become available as e-books.

Sent to Hell from Ann Arbor:
A College Student's World War One

Carl E.W. L. Dahlstrom, Ed. Rosalie V. Grafe. Portland, Oregon: Quaker Abbey Press, LLC, 2009, $16.95. Postage paid from quakerabbeypress. com.

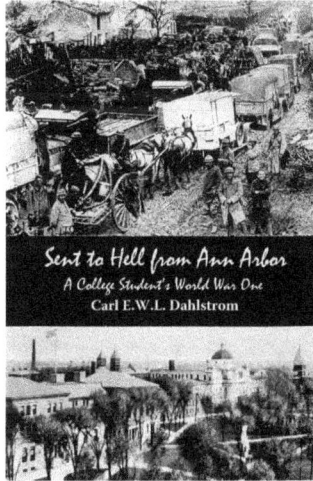

Michigan Historical Review, March 22, 2010, David Macleod

"Carl Dahlstrom (1897-1981) enlisted in the spring of 1918, in time to see battle that autumn as a soldier in the truck transport service in France and participate in the early occupation of Germany. Although the editor has supplied names of persons and places, family traditions, and a comprehensive index, the core of the book is Dahlstrom's autobiographical memoir, written entirely from memory shortly before the author's death. A vivid writer (he was a professor of English literature in the days before "theory" engulfed the field), Dahlstrom is bitter about the slaughter of ill-equipped and untrained American troops and the obtuseness of the high command. This is a thoughtful and very readable memoir that sets memories of wartime experience in the context of the author's family life, his boyhood and college years, and his changing sense of values."

Amigas del Senor
Methodist Monastery

Beth Blodgett (Sister Alegria) and Prairie Naoma Cutting (Sister Confianza), Rosalie V. Grafe, Ed., Quaker Abbel Press, LLC, Dec. 2010, 16.95 Postage paid from quakerabbeypress.com

Beth Blodgett and Prairie Naoma Cutting
(Sisters Alegría and Confianza)

From the Foreword by Sister Alberta Dieker, O.S.B. (Order of St. Benedict) Queen of Angels Monastery, author of *A Tree Rooted in Faith, A History of Queen of Angels Monastery.*

"Hermanas Alegria and Confianza are struggling to lead a religious life according to the spirit of the age-old monastic tradition. This tradition is based on a life lived in common, nurtured by daily prayer together, Scripture reading (lectio divina), goods shared in common, and meaningful work. The sisters make decisions according to the Quaker model, by prayer and discernment together. Their venture is unique since it began, not in the usual way as a foundation from an established monastery, but anew under the sponsorship of a Methodist community.

"This first-hand account of the experiences of these courageous women over the past two years makes for fascinating reading. One can laugh, or at least smile, at their misadventures. There are sad moments, too, as they encounter ignorance, poverty, and lack of medical and legal assistance for those who need it most. Their decision to live in voluntary poverty can lead the readers to assess their own attitudes toward possessions and abundance. Everyone can learn something from this story of a tenuous beginning which will certainly bear fruit in future and unknown ways."

Editor's Note: As of February, 2011, the monastery celebrated its fifth anniversary in Honduras.